HOW TO SELL
AND LIVE HAPPIER

For a complete list of Management Books 2000 titles,
visit our web-site at http://www.mb2000.com

HOW TO SELL YOUR BUSINESS AND LIVE HAPPILY EVER AFTER

Fifth Edition

Gary Morley

2000

First edition published 1997
Second edition published 1999
Third edition published 2003
Fourth edition published 2008
This new edition published 2010 by Management Books 2000 Ltd
Forge House, Limes Road
Kemble, Cirencester
Gloucestershire GL7 6AD
Tel: 01285 771441, Fax: 01285 771055
Website: www.mb2000.com Email: info@mb2000.com

British Library Cataloguing in Publication Data is available

ISBN 9781852526757

Whilst every effort has been made to ensure the accuracy of the contents
of this book, no responsibility can be accepted for any financial loss
resulting from action taken (or not taken) in reliance of its contents.

Preface

This book gives straightforward, practical advice on selling your business, including the tax implications, and is a comprehensive preparation for the complex issues involved. You will, of course, also need professional advice specific to your own case, but read what follows before you take any further steps, and use the book as an aide-mémoire during the selling process. Tell your advisers you are reading it – it will keep them on their toes!

Acknowledgements

I'd very much like to thank Guy Rigby for doing the proof reading and for his (unsolicited) comments, and to everyone else who helped towards making this book a success.

Contents

Introduction

Selling your business is probably the biggest financial undertaking of your life. You have only one chance to get it right. Getting it even slightly wrong can substantially affect your future.

As a business person, you may be faced with dozens of decisions every day, yet it is likely that all the decisions you make in the course of a year combined are less important than the right decision on selling your company.

First, what do you want to achieve? If your answer is, simply, "the biggest possible cheque", that's fine. But how would you feel if the existing operations were shut down, the name changed and the business transferred to some far-off enterprise zone? Would you have preferred the business to prosper relatively unchanged? Is it important to protect some or all of the employees? Do you want to remain involved on a part-time basis?

Knowing when to sell is also important. Few businesses show good profits over long periods. The perfect time to sell is usually when the profit cycle approaches its peak. It is therefore best to plan your intended sale well ahead.

How will you know if you have got the best possible price? There are many examples of companies being purchased and then sold soon afterwards at a huge profit. Also, if the highest price means having to wait for some of the money, the financial standing of the purchaser has to be considered – even highly respected public companies can suddenly go bust.

So you need to ensure that you achieve the best deal. You have no experience in valuing a business or negotiating a transaction with so many variables and which can be structured in so many different ways. The tax implications and the requirements of the Companies Acts are a labyrinth. And while all this is going on you have a business to run. How do you do it?

1

Appointing an Adviser

Never believe what you hear,
and only half believe what you see.

The first step is to appoint an advisor who will help with the technical side of things and steer you through the process with a mindful eye to the many potential pitfalls along the way. There are many professionals who claim to offer expertise in this area, ranging from county solicitors through to fully-fledged City merchant banks, and not all of them can always deliver the service you might expect.

One common method of trying to sell a business is by approaching the company's auditors or (even worse) the family solicitor. Most professional firms with under a hundred staff do not have Corporate Finance specialists. This, however, will not stop them from eagerly undertaking the assignment, as they believe it is relatively easy and it is their last chance to earn significant fees from a departing client!

Without a Corporate Finance specialist, the partner or manager undertaking the work will not have the experience either to market the business or to negotiate the best terms on your behalf. They will do some research into the obvious buyers of the business, and if that comes to nought (as it usually does), they flounder: they are trying to learn how to sell a business on the back of your fees. One of the biggest obstacles for Corporate Finance specialists in getting appointed is the complaint from the vendor that he has already spent considerable amounts of money by using his own accountant or solicitor, and has got nowhere. A poor intermediary can do harm: if there are time pressures on the vendor, some of that time has now been wasted; also, suitable purchasers have possibly been put off by badly handled approaches, and to approach them again would make you appear desperate.

Unless you enjoy paying large professional fees, never appoint anyone to act on the sale of your business who charges on a time basis. It is only in their interest to procrastinate, create unnecessary meetings and attend necessary meetings unnecessarily. "It's all good chargeable time" is a well-known professional phrase.

So how do you select an adviser?...

Track record: in a nutshell, this is what really matters. In the UK anyone can put a brass plate outside their door and advise on Mergers and Acquisitions – and it appears anyone does. If your intermediary does not have the right contacts and experience in doing deals, you will be wasting your time unless you (and he) are very lucky.

A good intermediary will have connections both in this country and overseas (especially in the EU and USA) with Merchant Banks, Corporate Finance specialists of the larger accountancy firms and other professional intermediaries. A good intermediary will know how to produce a good Information Memorandum; how to market a company confidentially; how to approach a prospective purchaser and reach the appropriate decision maker; how to present your business; how to identify time-wasters; and how to construct and deliver a short-list of interested, suitable and financially capable potential purchasers.

A good intermediary will have the ability and experience to overcome obstacles to the purchaser, either real or imagined, generated by the purchaser's solicitor. The purchaser's solicitor himself can usually also overcome these – if you are prepared to accept a lower price for your business!

Every intermediary will tell you, and probably very articulately, that he can do all the above and more. It is a case not of buyer beware, but of seller beware.

It is essential to meet with several intermediaries at their premises. This will allow you to judge their professionalism and choose the one you feel confident and comfortable with. You must meet and have your discussions with the person who would actually be doing the work. It is no good meeting the top man who may be authoritative and impressive in his presentation to you and who may be entitled "lead partner" or "controlling partner" but whom you would never see again. After the groundwork of finding potential buyers, the relationship between you and the intermediary can become very intense as important meetings become scheduled, and de-briefing sessions at your home or on the telephone late into the evening become common. The intermediary becomes aware of very personal details about you and your lifestyle – your wife's hobbies, what time you go to bed, what book your grand-daughter is reading. This level of closeness is inevitable, and therefore you must have confidence in your adviser. You don't have to like him, but you do have to trust him and be able to work with him.

When you meet the intermediary, you should obviously question him on his experience, on the experience of the Corporate Finance department and on his view of the prospects and methodology of getting a good price for your business; you should also get to know him as a person, because you are going to be working very closely with him. Questions should be searching. How many deals does he do each year? How many deals is he currently working on? How often has he been unable to find a suitable buyer? How long has he been in business? How did he become involved in corporate finance?

The intermediary with first-hand experience in the real world of making acquisitions and disposals will have a distinct advantage. He will better understand the motivations, fears and practical considerations of the purchaser. Being forearmed, he will be in a better position to take advantage of opportunities and overcome obstacles. Many professional advisers have for all their working lives only been advisers. They have no idea what it is like actually making the decision to spend a significant amount of their own or their company's money. It can be a very chastening experience. The adage "those who can, do; those who can't, teach" is very appropriate in the corporate finance profession.

Some intermediaries claim to be industry specialists, and you may feel more comfortable with someone who can speak your language and knows the jargon. The problem with industry specialists is that usually they know only the obvious buyers – whom you probably already know yourself – so if all they can do is approach those people to buy your business (with the attached inherent risks – see "Obvious purchasers", page 26), they are not contributing very much to the transaction. What you need is someone whose speciality is selling businesses, regardless of the particular sector concerned.

A very important consideration is that the intermediary is professionally qualified as an accountant or solicitor and that he is part of a substantial firm. This should ensure a minimum professional standard and to some extent be self-policing, since an established firm would not risk its reputation by having an incompetent adviser working on your behalf. It also allows for a firm of substance to be sued if things go wrong – particularly for poor tax advice.

Another good indicator of a quality firm is that it is

authorised and regulated by the Financial Services Authority ("FSA"). As well as giving the firm the ability to provide certain services or advice that other firms are prohibited by law from providing, it also means that each of the partners, directors and executives have been individually approved by the FSA as "fit and proper" persons. All firms authorised by the FSA must state that on their letterheads and literature.

Think very carefully, also, about the solicitor you are going to use. Many people, even experienced business people, think every solicitor has a thorough understanding of every aspect of the law. It just ain't so! Solicitors specialise, like other professionals. If you were going blind you would be referred to an eye specialist. Your friend, the eminent heart surgeon, wouldn't come into it, but neither would he want to – and that is the difference! There are many specialist solicitors: those in banking law, in international shipping law, in franchise law, and of course in corporate law, but the danger is that if you go to your own solicitor – the family friend who did your house conveyancing and prepared your will – he will express himself as only too glad to act for you in a matter on which he has absolutely no experience. This can cost dearly. Inexperienced solicitors do not always protect their clients' best interests because not only might they miss an important point (and the purchaser's experienced corporate lawyer can quickly smell inexperience on the other side and milk it for all it's worth), but they might also argue *ad nauseam* over some incidental point that any reasonable corporate solicitor would accept without question, with obvious implications for your ultimate costs. In such circumstances it is not uncommon for your legal fees to be greater than those of the purchaser – and it is his solicitor who has to draw up the contract and undertake all the legal due diligence. It has also been known for the purchasers to withdraw out of frustration at not being able to come to a reasonable Sale and Purchase Agreement with an obstinate (for invalid reasons) solicitor. If you want to be properly protected, remember the advantages of using an experienced corporate lawyer.

Fees

Everything is negotiable. Haggle if you want to, although it will be far cheaper in the long run to get the right intermediary at seemingly higher fees than a bad intermediary at lower ones. Don't be tempted to use an intermediary who will act for you for nothing, stating that he will get the fee from the purchaser. The maxim "There's no such thing as a free lunch" is oh, so true of advisers! Obviously the purchaser will not pay any more, overall, than he thinks the business is worth to him, so if he has to pay the intermediary he will pay you less. But, more importantly, if the intermediary has a financial arrangement with the purchaser he will be acting in his interest rather than in yours. Worse still, from his perspective the selling of your business becomes a numbers game – he will want to place your details in front of as many people as possible, with the result that you will waste a considerable amount of time and energy seeing unsuitable purchasers. Such intermediaries need have little regard to the quality of their advice when this happens; and that means you are the loser.

The intermediary's fees should be substantially success-orientated. If they aren't, forget it. If the intermediary does not have faith in his ability to deliver, how can you?

By and large, fees in the industry work to the "Lehman Scale" – 5% of the first million pounds paid, 4% of the next, 3% of the third, 2% of the fourth, and 1% of anything above. In addition, there is usually a relatively small monthly retainer paid to the intermediary. This will not represent anything close to the time costs of the intermediary, but is in reality a commitment fee. The owner of a business might appoint an intermediary on a success-only basis, then, when it comes to the crunch with an offer on the table, change his mind and turn it down. This would be unfair on the intermediary, who would have done a lot of work for nothing. Also, if another client who was paying a retainer had demands which conflicted with yours, there would be a moral and practical obligation to put the paying client first, and with several paying clients, your requirements would have a low priority. Not only can the refusal to pay a retainer be a false economy, but you should be very dubious about appointing any intermediary who will work without such a commitment fee – he is obviously all too desperate for your business.

Advice on the taxation aspects of the sale are sometimes included in the success fee and should come only from a professionally qualified person – and you should always get it in writing.

One last thought – if you think professional fees can cost a lot, try out the amateur variety!

2

Preparing for Sale

Life is what happens to you while you are making plans for it.

Think long and hard about what you want to achieve from selling your business. It is worth spending time on this. You may want to discuss it over several months with your spouse, fellow directors and minority shareholders.

You are facing the biggest financial decision of your life. You need to plan it. You need to know what you will do with the money. You need to know what you will do afterwards; even perhaps what your spouse is going to do. Only then can you be properly advised on how to achieve it. Once you have established your criteria, you can then start doing what is necessary.

With only a little foresight you can change some of the things that you do or don't do within your business, and thereby enhance its value. Longer-term planning can enhance its value still further. A number of possible courses of action are set out below. Of course, you don't have to do any of the things suggested – it's your business, and your money!

The quickest way to improve profitability is to stop any

"private" expenditure. This could be your private plane, your mother-in-law's Mercedes (or Mini), the gardener, "business" trips or the dining out. It is possible to explain all these things to a prospective purchaser, but then they will have to be itemised and agreed upon. It also means "washing your dirty linen in public". The sooner you stop the perks the better. There have been cases where the former owners of a business were sued to pay back expenditure of this kind as they are not true business expenses.

You should pay yourself as if you were an employee, at a rate commensurate with your position. This does not mean you have to lower your standard of living – you can simply switch to paying monthly dividends. The tax differential between salary and dividends is now fairly minimal, but this will boost the reported profits of your company. The viability of paying dividends will depend on who owns the shares. If you (and your spouse) don't own them all you will need the minority shareholders to agree to waive their rights to these extra dividends which are being paid to increase the value of their shares.

If your company qualifies you should consider re-registering your company as a PLC (it basically means a minimum of £50,000 distributable reserves and share capital). This gives an impression of success and stability. Even if you decide not to sell, the effect on customers, suppliers, competitors and staff will still be of benefit. The requirements are not onerous, and the direct costs of registering should be below £500. You will also have the additional costs of reprinting stationery and promotional material.

You should use the audited accounts as a showcase for your business. Don't take advantage of any of the reduced reporting requirements. Include a Chairman's Statement – expand the definition of Principal Activity in the Directors' Report – boast about what you have achieved and where the company is going. Freehold property (and other significant fixed assets) should be revalued, if appropriate, to reflect their enhanced value. Sell any redundant assets. If you are planning far enough ahead, write off any goodwill in your balance sheet so that it does not affect profits at the time of the sale.

The accounting policies should be reviewed to report maximum profits. This is often the opposite of what a family company tries to achieve to mitigate tax.

The controls and measurement of company performance should become formalised. You should implement budgetary controls and management accounts and ideally have several years' practice at this before selling, so that you know where your business is and the direction it is taking. This is particularly important if you sell your business on an "earn-out", where a proportion of the consideration is paid later on the basis of future profits. It will also help to demonstrate the underlying potential of the business to a prospective purchaser.

You should also at an early stage remove any dead wood including poorly performing staff. Apart from the obvious benefit to the company, a new owner will do it anyway, and it may affect earn-out calculations. You may feel it is better for all concerned for you to come to an arrangement now with staff who the company has outgrown rather than leaving them to be dismissed by the new owner with minimum compensation.

Give staff proper titles for the jobs they are doing. Have meetings and decisions minuted. This shows that there is management, structure and control in the business.

As with most things in life, presentation can be more important than content. How your company is presented can have an inordinate effect on how much purchasers will pay for it.

Finally, make sure that the shareholding structure of the company is as simple as possible. Minority interests, in particular, should be taken out wherever possible. By and large, purchasers do not like the inconvenience of having minority shareholders, and will therefore want to acquire one hundred per cent of the company. There can be difficulties in having to deal with several vendors and the need to come to decisions acceptable to all. The other shareholders may have a different set of objectives from yours. The minority shareholders, if they are employed in the business, may want an "executive style" ongoing employment contract which would be expensive for the new owners to break – this reduces the value of the business to the purchasers, and the burden falls disproportionately on you. It may be that the minority shareholders are not dependent on the sale proceeds. In such circumstances it has been known for them to demand a higher price for their shares, as they know you need to sell, and if this is not forthcoming they might veto a sale. The purchaser isn't going to pay more for the company and, in such circumstances, you are the one who will have to cough up.

If potential conflict with minority shareholders does exist, then before negotiations begin with any prospective purchaser you would be strongly advised to obtain a legally binding option from them for a period of, say, eighteen months, to allow you to purchase their shares and re-sell them on the same terms as you are selling your own. This is a no-gain-no-loss arrangement, but it allows you to deliver one hundred per cent of the share capital to a purchaser.

The Companies Acts do allow minority shareholdings of under ten per cent in total to be compulsorily purchased in a takeover, but the legal costs make this prohibitively expensive other than in large deals, and the purchaser would expect you to foot the bill.

If differing objectives do exist between the shareholders, a compromise could be achieved. For example, the deal could be structured so that the director/shareholders participate in an earn-out while the passive shareholders take a higher proportion of the initial consideration. Where there is goodwill between the shareholders, an experienced intermediary should be able to produce a satisfactory settlement for all concerned.

3

Finding a Purchaser

God save me from my friends;
from my enemies I can save myself.

There are several ways of going about finding a purchaser:

- Advertising
- Approaching competitors
- Approaching suppliers or distributors who may be interested in "vertical integration"
- Approaching individual or corporate investors who might have an interest in adding your company to their portfolio
- Looking for overseas purchasers interested in territorial expansion

Advertising

You might think, once you have decided to sell your business, that a cheap and easy way to start would be to place a simple newspaper advertisement. This probably spells disaster!

This is how things can go wrong if you advertise. You are inundated with enquiries: they come from competitors (usually in disguise); people with no money; corporate vultures; time-wasters; second-rate intermediaries who suspect you need help and want to capitalise on your naivety; and, just possibly, genuine potential purchasers. You don't know what to do. You try to pick out the best respondents, you meet several and waste a lot of time. This takes you away from managing your business, which costs you money. Your staff become concerned at the parade of visitors to your premises. Your chief accountant twigs that something is afoot when he receives repeated requests for information from different visitors, which leads him to conclude that you must be selling the business. The cat is out of the bag. Once one person within a company knows, everyone knows.

Staff do not like the uncertainty of change. They don't know who they will be working for, or whether they may be made redundant. Your best people (and especially your good salespeople) may start applying for jobs with your competitors, who quickly learn their reasons for wanting to leave. Your competitors tell their salesmen, who in turn tell your customers, that you are having to sell out because: (a) you are going bust and/or the bank is no longer willing to support you, and therefore you cannot be relied upon for deliveries; (b) you have to sell to settle gambling debts or to meet calls from the several Lloyds syndicates to which you belong; (c) you are going to emigrate to San Francisco with a young boy from the tennis club; or (d) you've got a social disease...

However it is put, it will give your competitors an edge, as by this time they have taken on your sales staff, and your customers will want a reliable supplier.

The loss of staff, and the low morale of those who remain, will affect your business. This, together with the amount of your time taken up meeting the respondents to the advertisement can have a dire effect – within a short time your monthly management accounts show worsening results and any genuine prospective purchaser thinks you are selling out just before the bubble bursts. Not the best climate in which to secure a good deal.

Almost as a knee-jerk reaction, many people do place an advertisement in *The Financial Times* to try to sell their business. This is an excellent newspaper, but it is not the place to sell a business. Most of the companies advertised for sale there are in receivership. In these cases it does not matter what the staff or competitors think: it's too late for that. It is doubtful whether many businesses advertised in *The Financial Times* – other than those in receivership – end up with the best deal for the vendor.

Flotation

Some sellers of business are led into believing that the best way to achieve a successful sale is by floating it on the Stock Exchange or junior markets such as AIM (Alternative Investment Market) or PLUS. This is anything but a sale. If what you want to achieve is simply a small percentage of the value of your business in hard cash and to continue working hard then flotation may, and only may, be appropriate. The downsides to such a route are:

(a) Your fortunes and that of your business are subject to the vagaries of stock market sentiment as a whole and therefore out of your control: for example, Monsoon plc floated (on the main London Stock Exchange) in February 1998 at a price of 195p per share – announced their financial results in September 1998 which were exactly as they had forecast when they floated – and the shares were valued 65% lower at 67p.

(b) After the flotation it will be difficult for you to raise any further significant money from the sale of your shares without disastrously affecting the share price (unless you sell all of your remaining holding).

(c) It is never certain that the vast amount of legal, financial and management work involved in grooming the company will actually result in a flotation. This can waste a substantial amount of your time and money, as well as demoralising for your staff and potentially damaging the value of the company should you then want to sell it.

(d) You and your top management will have to spend time on "City" matters that have nothing to do with your business. You will also have to brief stock market analysts and explain your results and decisions in far more detail than you have done to anyone in the past. Your company will be constantly scrutinised so that any mistake will be made public for all to see. Even removing a director of the company will have to be considered in the context of how it will be interpreted by the "City".

(e) The business will have to incur significant additional costs each year producing glossy financial statements, employing more expensive auditors, financial PR consultants etc.

(f) You must continue to show significant profit growth year after year or become "dead stock".

Flotation is an ideal route in specific circumstances but definitely not if your objectives are to secure your financial future or for you and your family to enjoy the spoils of your success.

Obvious purchasers

An "obvious" purchaser for your business is one who operates in the same or a similar business, whether vertically or horizontally. You know of him, and he probably knows of you. An obvious purchaser is usually either a competitor or a potential competitor.

Such potential purchasers could be good news. They will already understand your business, causing less disruption in getting to know it and making lower demands on your time. The potential for cost savings which could be made on a takeover will be more apparent (and probably more obtainable) to them, and therefore they may be able to pay a higher price. They will probably be able to eliminate some overheads, such as the accounts department, or even the General Manager. Depending on the rationale for their interest, they may be able to eliminate selling costs by using their own sales force to sell your product along with their own. They may want to utilise your spare capacity by shifting their production to your premises, thereby saving on the rent and rates of premises that they vacate. There may be economies of scale in production or in bulk buying power. Clearly, most businesses will have very great attractions to an obvious purchaser.

However, obvious purchasers may not be willing to pay you a premium for the savings that they are going to make. The reverse is often true: most obvious purchasers will know your weaknesses and play on them – this is particularly true if they are aware of pressures on you to sell. Direct competitors will probably already know who your major customers are, who your suppliers are and how your company operates. Why should they pay a premium for it? They may believe, particularly in a business that operates in a niche market, that they are the only potential purchasers because they have checked out any other obvious purchasers. In such circumstances it is unlikely that they are going to make a generous offer. It is therefore dangerous to your wealth to limit the marketing of your business solely to obvious purchasers.

Because obvious purchasers will usually be competitors, the releasing of commercial information to them must be of serious concern. Even the very fact that the company is for sale can cause it irreparable damage. Notwithstanding that the competitor has signed a confidentiality undertaking this can not in practice stop a whispering campaign, and the onus of proof of any breach of confidentiality would be on you.

A further major disadvantage of directing the sale of your business only to obvious purchasers is that it unnecessarily limits your options. There are many potential purchasers whom you could not possibly know, each with their own criteria or acquisition – and your company may fit these criteria. Confidential professional marketing of your business by a good intermediary should provide you with a short-list of active acquirers who want to buy your business.

A couple of examples will probably best illustrate the point:

i) A computer software company purchased a double-glazing window manufacturer. The reason: The computer software company had sold its business and assets (as opposed to selling the shares). This meant that for tax purposes it was advantageous for it to buy a business that had freehold premises and substantial plant and equipment (so it could roll-over the gain and defer paying tax). The owner of the company was really a sales-orientated person who had "fallen into" the software business. He saw the potential that the double-glazing window manufacturer would have with a stronger sales and marketing approach. He could provide that strength and the tax would also be saved, so his company bought the business.

ii) A council services contractor sold its business to a medium-sized quoted healthcare company. The contractor knew all the obvious purchasers, but for reasons of confidentiality appointed an intermediary to front the situation, supplying him with a list of their names. The contractor ideally wanted £4m. None of the obvious purchasers were interested as it was too expensive. The intermediary introduced the quoted healthcare company, who paid £9m. The reason: the quoted company needed both to diversify and to improve the quality of its earnings; the contractor had good profitable contracts with councils for up to five years ahead, and the price paid was lower than its P/E ratio and therefore did not dilute its earnings per share.

There is of course nothing wrong in selling your business to an obvious purchaser, but the relative risks must be weighed against the possible rewards.

Management Buy-Outs

Another big danger is trying to sell your business to your own staff – commonly known as a Management Buy-Out ("MBO"). Whilst it is true that there are many successful high profile MBOs where the value of the deal is in excess of £50 million, what isn't widely known is the disastrous effects that can occur when owners of smaller companies begin to negotiate with their key staff who want to buy their businesses.

Immediately, the loyal and dedicated staff you have known for years suddenly have goals that are opposite to yours. They do not want to maximise the value of the business to you; they want to minimise it for them. It is in their interest to reduce profitability (in the short term) and thus reduce the price. You have created the "Enemy Within".

The danger of the Enemy Within cannot be overstated. Once the possibility of riches beyond their dreams takes hold, even your most decent and upright member of staff can, and often does, become unscrupulous. The whole management team can become unscrupulous. It is their big chance. The following is a true story:

A large diverse private group decided to have a more focussed direction. The management of one of the subsidiaries (which was in security and access control) saw what was happening and began, in a very ruthless way, to turn the profits into losses. They even made the gross profit into a loss! They then made an offer to buy the company. The holding company knew something was amiss but not what. The holding company decided, as a point of principle that they would not sell the company to the management team; who then left. The company, void of any management, was sold to a competitor for £1. The new owner put his accounting systems in place and discovered undervalued stocks and work in progress and substantial under invoicing; he found in excess of £500,000 which he did not expect to receive!

Even if you have absolute faith in the integrity of your staff, that only overcomes one of the impediments to a successful MBO. You will have several parties with whom you have to negotiate.

First, there is the management team. This is not usually the easiest of discussions. You will clearly be extolling the virtues of the company and its very bright future, whilst your staff will be putting to you its shortcomings and other hard-hitting home truths. Can you imagine having such a meeting with your three most senior managers and how it would affect the ongoing management of the business?

Also, it is not uncommon for the MBO team to have disagreements between themselves and fall out; that also does not help with the ongoing management of the business. The MBO team will need to have a deal agreed, in broad terms, before they can start the arduous exercise of actually raising the money to fund the purchase.

Except for very small deals, the funding will invariably come from Venture Capitalists ("VCs"). VC funds now like to be known as Private Equity providers probably because it sounds softer and easier to deal with, and the word venture can easily be mistaken for the word vulture! They are, however, still as shrewd and as calculating as ever.

Once the VCs are involved they will virtually always want

to renegotiate the deal – and *not* (surprise, surprise) in your favour! At this stage it will be impossible to get alternative competitive bids from trade buyers as meetings with the MBO team will hardly be conducive to a positive view on the suitability and value of the proposed acquisition.

The MBO team may, at an early stage, produce a letter from a VC purporting to support the deal. Read the letter clearly and you will see it means nothing more than that the VC is happy to look at the proposal or any other proposal that may come along. Some VCs issue these letters to prospective MBO teams before the initial approach to the owners. It is not and cannot be regarded as any commitment at all.

VCs will not commit to funding a deal unless they are fully satisfied with a) the terms of the deal with you, b) the soundness of the business, c) the abilities of the management team and d) the terms of their deal with the management team.

On these points, VCs much prefer to back a team rather than an individual. They like to see that the team has the skills of leadership, finance, sales and operations. VCs also have a requirement that each member of the team puts some of his own money at risk in funding the deal. This "hurt" money is useful a) as an indication of commitment to the deal and b) to tie them into the deal so that they have the same objectives as the VCs and makes it difficult for them to leave the venture. The hurt money can usually only come from one source: remortgaging the family home. No matter how gung-ho the MBO team member might be in becoming his own boss, his spouse can take a very different view of risk when she has to sign away the family home.

Many MBO teams (as well as the vendors of the business) do not realise at the outset that a substantial part of any VC funds used for an MBO are lent to the business as secured loans which attract interest. The result is a highly geared business which means that for the next 3 to 7 years virtually all the profits generated by the business are used to fund the interest and capital repayments on the loans.

It is a fact that less than 10% of proposals put to VCs actually result in a deal. So, possibly through no fault of their own, the MBO team fail in their bid for your business – it will have taken up a considerable amount of time and money from your most key staff. How now will the business have been affected? How demotivated and demoralised will your key staff be? How now will an outside prospective purchaser view the value of your business?

You have been warned.

Less obvious purchasers

Finding less obvious purchasers is much more difficult, and this is where a good intermediary with expertise in mergers and acquisitions, and a network of active contacts, can be particularly useful. Often these kind of transactions develop on the basis of word-of-mouth – with contact made through informal or "networked" channels.

An experienced intermediary will have a host of different contacts and potential purchasers simply by being in the business of mergers and acquisitions. Acquisitive individuals and companies are in constant contact with merger and acquisition specialists to ensure that should a suitable target become available, then they will have an early opportunity to consider it.

The titanic expansion of the Alternative Investment Market ("AIM") and the smaller and less regulated PLUS market has created a plethora of companies that sorely need to use their (relatively) highly rated quoted shares to make acquisitions. It is the way of the stock markets that unless a company produces above average growth then the value of its shares drops like a stone into the abyss, often never to return. Acquisitions are a classic method of producing growth. So here is a potential fountain of possible purchasers but unless you are connected to them or their stockbrokers it is unlikely that you will know who might be suitable to acquire your business.

Research

If you are insistent on doing the spadework yourself there are several sources of information – sometimes overlapping, sometimes complimentary.

Most large libraries have directories of businesses, such as Kompass, which list businesses both by geographical location and by commercial activity. Such directories are better at some industry sectors than at others – check to see whether your business is listed.

If you think that your business may be suited to a quoted company, then McCarthys is useful for finding out the latest information. The larger public libraries often have the latest annual report and financial statements of quoted companies – useful to find out the name of the chairman or financial director to contact.

Don't forget Yellow Pages – also often found in the larger public libraries. Also trade journals/magazines for your industry often report on who's acquired who – but be careful not to limit your search to "obvious" sectors only (see above).

The national company search agents such as Infocheck and Dun & Bradstreet can do searches on information held at Companies House using criteria such as turnover, postcodes and the standard industry classification (SIC) code on the annual return.

The accountancy firm, KPMG, and the magazine Acquisitions Monthly produce lists of recent acquisitions and disposals showing, inter alia, the size of the deals and the parties concerned. This may be a good starting point but by the very nature of such lists not all transactions are reported.

If you are on the Internet – well, the world is your lobster. You can spend many afternoons and evenings surfing away amassing huge amounts of data. A good place to start is www.google.com, particularly the advanced search facility which allows you to pinpoint what you are looking for.

However, never forget that no matter how thorough and detailed your research is, you will only ever be identifying companies which *you* think may be interested in acquiring you. You will not produce a list of potential purchasers who *themselves* think they are interested in acquiring you. Companies who you think should be interested may not actually be interested at all, while there may well be potential purchasers out there who have their own reasons for being interested in acquiring you which you could not begin to anticipate!

Making the approach

In most instances an approach from a professional intermediary has a better chance of success than a cold approach from the vendor in person – for much the same reason that a publisher will be more receptive to a proposal from a literary agent than from an unpublished author. The fact that a professional intermediary has endorsed the proposal by taking it on in the first place adds weight to the proposal itself; the indirect approach also enables a potential investor (or publisher) to assess the proposal without fear of being dragged into a difficult personal correspondence if the proposal is rejected.

Obviously there are exceptions to this rule; where the target is already known personally to the vendor, it clearly makes sense to build on this existing relationship with a direct approach. However, it can still be advantageous to hand over the grittier aspects of negotiations to a third party.

Confidentiality undertaking

Whichever way you find a potential buyer it is essential that you get an appropriate confidentiality undertaking from them before divulging any information. An intermediary would be able to get a confidentiality undertaking prior to them even knowing the name of your company. Do not think that such an undertaking will protect your business from unscrupulous operators (so always be cautious in revealing information) but it is far better to have one than not.

Appendix IV gives an example of a confidentiality undertaking.

4

The Information Memorandum

Even hot cakes have to be sold.

The Information Memorandum, sometimes called a prospectus, is normally prepared by the intermediary as part of his overall service, and included in his fee.

The Information Memorandum is primarily a selling document. It should present your business in the most favourable way, highlighting its strengths and minimising its weaknesses. It should also be comprehensive enough to answer all the questions a prospective purchaser needs to ask. This will save you time, as you will then meet only those who have made a serious decision to take matters further. A good Information Memorandum will help reduce staff unease by significantly reducing the number of clandestine meetings the Chairman has with people who are never heard of again.

For it to be useful, the Information Memorandum must inevitably contain a great deal of confidential information about your company. You may be reluctant to release such information, even to your intermediary. But a good intermediary will be able to produce an effective Information

Memorandum without divulging any potentially damaging information. It may be that fifteen per cent of your turnover is derived from one customer – an important fact to a potential purchaser which should be disclosed early – but the Information Memorandum does not have to name the customer.

All the information contained in the Memorandum must be approved by you for inclusion. The best way to achieve the balance between producing a meaningful Information Memorandum and not disclosing potentially damaging information is for you to provide all the information to the intermediary, for him to draft the memorandum, and for you to check the draft. Then no information will be disclosed to third parties without your explicit approval.

Although written up by the intermediary, virtually all the information must be provided by your company. A sample list of information required is set out in Appendix I. This list will vary for different types of business. Once this information is assembled, further points will be raised.

The Information Memorandum will also restate the profit history, adjusting for "personal" expenses and non-recurrent items. It would be preferable, however, that such expenses did not exist in the first place, rather than needing explanation to sceptical potential purchasers.

The intermediary will have his own format for the Information Memorandum. It must have clarity and be user friendly – surprisingly uncommon attributes. It should at the beginning have an "executive summary" explaining in brief terms what the business is and why it is an opportunity not to be missed.

The body of the Information Memorandum will have sections such as:-

History and Background
- How the business started
- Who started it
- Major developments
- Key influences
- The market place
- Unique Selling Points (USPs)
- Strengths and weaknesses
- Who owns it now
- Why it is up for sale

Sales
- Types of product
- Product sales profile
- Types of customers
- Customer sales profile
- Significant customers
- How customers are serviced
- Terms of business
- Competitors
- Sales structure
- Sales incentives
- Promotional activities

Operations
- Manufacturing process
- Buying process
- Components/raw material profile
- Supplier profile
- Stockholding policies
- Major items of plant and equipment

Premises

- Location
- Descriptions
- Activities at each location
- Lease details
- Valuations

Management and Staff

- Structure and organisation chart
- CVs for directors and senior management
- Skill requirements
- Awards or memberships
- Who would be leaving on a change of ownership
- Employment details for each category of staff:
  - Pay levels
  - Performance related pay
  - Share options
  - Holidays
  - Notice periods
  - Cars
  - Pensions
  - Insurances
  - Other benefits
  - Restrictive covenants

Financials

- Full actual historic
- Detailed forecasts
- Analysis of "true" profit history
- Description of extraordinary and exceptional items
- Explanation of unusual balance sheet items
- Details of possible synergistic savings
- Details of any assets or liabilities not being included in the sale

- Details of borrowings including HP, leasing and personal guarantees
- Details of any unusual or onerous agreements not mentioned elsewhere

Never forget that the Information Memorandum is a selling document.

Financial projections

The financial forecasts are probably the most important part of the Information Memorandum. It is what the potential purchasers are buying: the future. You may think you are selling the past results of your business, but no, those results only put into context your projections of what is going to happen in the future. A considerable part of the effort a potential purchaser will put into evaluating your business will be on scrutinising "the numbers". Therefore, too much thought and consideration cannot be applied in producing them.

A good intermediary will advise you on the format, detail and periods to be covered by the projections that are appropriate to your business. Indeed, a good intermediary should play devil's advocate to make sure the numbers stack-up and that the assumptions are realistic and robust.

Once a potential purchaser is satisfied with the overall feel of the prospective acquisition it is then that his accountants will examine and question in depth the forecasts. If, in their opinion, the forecasts look unreliable (or, as it is referred to in technospeak, rubbish) their interest will stop there and then. For you, this is a total waste of time and opportunity. Properly prepared and presented forecasts (which may well have given the same financial results) would have given them the confidence to proceed.

So what are the things to look out for? As a minimum there should be profit and loss accounts identifying the major sources of revenue and expenditure; detailed cashflow projections for the same periods and balance sheets which must tie together the profit and loss accounts and cashflow projections and reconcile back to the latest audited accounts. And, just as important as all the above combined, are the assumptions. It is the assumptions that tell whether the projections are viable, realistic, pessimistic, optimistic or codswollop. Assumptions are things that you don't know: but you must know why you think the assumption you have made is correct. You will be asked to explain and justify them.

A common mistake is to forget seasonality within the business and an even bigger mistake is to give a forecast that looks like it's a dog's leg! It is very difficult for financial projections to have any credibility when they show good, steady historic growth and then, as soon as the business is for sale, lo and behold, the year after you depart sales are forecast to double and profits treble! Life (and business) is not like that. The effect of including such projections (apart from generating mild hilarity) is that it taints the whole of the Information Memorandum as wishful thinking and therefore something not to be taken seriously.

Some Information Memoranda include a "sensitivity analysis" in their financial projections, showing how the results vary if the principal assumptions are changed. Whilst this is useful when trying to raise funds, on the sale of a business it is probably more appropriate to let the prospective purchaser's accountants carry this out as part of their due diligence exercise.

Appendix III provides a set of sample financial projections, to show how they might appear in attachment to the Information Memorandum.

Confidentiality

Before the Information Memorandum is released to any potential purchaser, the intermediary should obtain specific clearance from you that that particular person may receive it.

The intermediary should obtain from the potential purchaser a written confidentiality undertaking, and also ensure that he has the financial ability to conclude the acquisition.

Sample information memorandum

A sample information memorandum is set out in Appendix II. This is provided for illustrative purposes only to give readers an idea of how the memorandum might look when presented to prospective purchasers. The actual contents and presentation of the memorandum will vary widely according to the particular characteristics and circumstances of the company in question.

5

Price

Value, like beauty, is in the eye of the beholder.

You have been made an offer. It may not be what you had been hoping for, but it is nevertheless a good price. Only you can decide whether (a) to accept the offer; (b) to try to renegotiate; or (c) to keep the business on the market. And only you know the consequences of not accepting an offer in your own particular circumstances – whether of flourishing business, deteriorating business, your own age, failing health, pressure from the bank, family needs or whatever other reasons you have for selling.

The valuation of a business works on imperfect information. It is not like selling a house in a street of similar houses, in which case you know what the one down the road sold for a couple of months ago. There is no other business the same as yours in the same location and of similar size. Even if there were, how would you know its value?

There are no rules to tell you what your business is worth. There is no such thing as a "correct" price. A business can be worth twice as much to one person as to another – and neither will be wrong – or necessarily right for you. And note that if you have had a share valuation agreed by Inland Revenue Share Valuation, do not think that that is even an approximation of the real value of your business. The valuation by the Inland Revenue is merely a value agreed between them and your tax advisers based on a rigid set of rules used only for tax collection purposes. It has little to do with the best price that someone may be prepared to pay in the real world. Happily, an Inland Revenue agreed valuation is usually lower than an actual selling price.

There are in fact a number of different indicators used by the investment community for the purposes of valuation, as further referred to below, but remember that the purchaser is likely to have his own unique approach to valuing your business which will take into account his own preferences rather than any objective measure of valuation.

It is also worth noting that even the experts can get it wrong. For example, Boots the chemist disastrous acquisition of Do-It-All cost the UK's biggest pharmacy chain £400 million over nine painful years. And Ford bought Kwik-Fit for £1bn in 1999 and sold it in 2002 for a value of £407m. How many decisions cost £200m per annum? Then there is the Grand-daddy of them all: Marconi spent so much on wrong acquisitions, the value of the company dropped from over £3bn to under £50m. Obviously neither the directors of these companies nor their highly-paid City advisers thought that they were paying too much at the time. On the other hand, the Ladbroke Group's acquisition of Hilton Hotels in the 1980s was highly criticised at the time only to be later roundly endorsed.

In the final analysis, however, risk is what the price is all about. A purchaser could put his money in a building society, earn interest on it and know it is guaranteed by the Bank of England. What makes an acquisition more viable is that it should produce a much better overall rate of return. The more risky a venture, the higher the rate of return that is required – otherwise no one would take on the additional risk. The corollary is that the higher the rate of return required, the lower the price will be. It is the assessment of the risk which will value your business. This assessment is not a science; it is an art.

At the end of the day it all boils down to a question of earnings, and the purchaser's required rate of return on capital invested in your business – and, of course, the premium he is prepared to pay (for whatever reason) for the privilege. This obviously makes it hard, if not impossible, to predict the outcome before embarking on the selling process, but here is a list of the considerations likely to affect the price you will ultimately receive:

Asset backing

Whilst few companies are valued by reference to their assets (with the obvious exception of property companies), the underlying asset value of a business nevertheless provides an important element of comfort (or otherwise) which will influence the price a purchaser may be prepared to pay. The more net assets a purchaser gets for his money, and the less debt within the company, the more attractive it will be.

One obvious implication of the asset value is that it defines the maximum downside for the purchaser – being the difference between what he is paying and the asset value of what he is acquiring.

A second important consideration is the accounting treatment of the "goodwill" arising on the acquisition (the difference between purchase price and asset value). This has either to be written off immediately, creating a dent in the assets of the acquirer, or written off over a number of years against the profits of the acquirer (such write-offs being non-tax deductible). Of course, this is more relevant to quoted companies than to private companies or individuals.

The availability of asset backing can be an important element in helping the purchaser put together his funding arrangements for the acquisition. For example, he may wish to factor the debts, or mortgage the freehold property to create extra cash.

Barriers to entry

The more barriers to entry the better. The more difficult it is for others to get into your market and compete with you, the higher the value of your business. A barrier to entry could be large set-up costs, as for example in car manufacturing, or the need for international distribution centres and personnel. It could be a technical barrier, such as patents or the need for government licences, as with television franchises. It could be a physical limitation, such as "slots" at Heathrow airport. It could be market dominance. Whatever the barriers to entry, they give an element of security to a potential purchaser, and also prevent him thinking that he could start up an equally profitable competitive operation at a lower net cost than the price you want for your business.

Break-up value

This is the value that would be left, net of tax, if the business were closed down, the assets sold and the creditors paid off. This value rarely has anything to do with the net asset value as shown in your audited accounts. Usually the break-up value is lower, as your accounts will be prepared on a "going concern" basis which ignores the redundancy costs of closing a business and the discount on the stock value if it were sold as a job lot. Leasehold premises may also need to be written down to create a "negative value" if a premium has to be paid to the landlord to cancel the lease.

Sometimes the break-up value can be higher than the value shown in the accounts. This can occur where assets (such as freehold land or major items of plant and machinery) are shown in the accounts at their historic cost less depreciation, whereas their market value is now significantly higher. In the 1960s and 1970s in particular, Jim Slater and others made their fortunes by recognising that some businesses were under-performing and that the true value of the underlying assets bore no relationship to the figures shown in the audited accounts. They bought the companies, closed many of them down and sold off their assets, often at a vast profit. This technique is known as "asset-stripping". If you unknowingly sell a business for less than its break-up value, you have been very badly advised.

Cash flow

Businesses generating cash are more desirable than cash-hungry businesses for three obvious reasons. First, cash-hungry businesses require ongoing funding. Second, there is an inbuilt uncertainty with these businesses concerning the point at which they may start to yield distributable surpluses. And third, in the case of cash-generating businesses, these have the significant advantage of being able to assist in the repayment of any financing costs relating to the acquisition.

Some businesses require extra cash in order to grow, while others produce excess cash as they grow. A good example of the former is leasing companies: the profit margins are generally not large, and therefore retained profits cannot produce the funds necessary to generate very much new business. To produce a further £100 of profit may require, for example a further £1500 to be invested (though naturally the leases eventually become cash-positive). An example of a "cash cow" is exhibition-organising companies, which generate cash as exhibitors pay in advance: therefore, as more exhibitions are organised (i.e. the business is expanding), more exhibitors pay in advance, generating more cash.

Some acquirers will actually use the cash flow projections to provide a basis for valuation, using a method known as "discounted cash flow" (DCF) analysis. This is a technique designed to discount the projected stream of cash flows at the investor's required rate of return (the "discount rate"), to calculate their "net present value". This approach is popular among business schools and certain sections of the financial community. It is more commonly used for project evaluation than company valuation but can nevertheless provide a useful indicator of underlying value in a business.

One criticism is that it does not recognise the premium certain buyers will pay for a business.

Dependency

If your business is heavily dependent on something or someone, then its profits are at risk. The dependency could be, for example, the personal loyalty shown by major customers or suppliers to the Chairman. This will probably cause serious problems if the Chairman is to leave the company at or shortly after the sale. The dependency could be on a supplier who accounts for (say) eighty per cent of purchases; if the supplier were to go bust, or have an irresolvable altercation with your company, production and credit terms could be badly affected. The situation is mirrored by dependency on one customer, or a small number of customers. Dependency could also be on a niche, which, although it might have been there for decades and even be protected by patents or legislation, can still disappear. An example of such a business would have been the supplier of the drinking vessels used by the Royal Navy to dispense their tots of rum! Dependency could be the utilisation of a specific process or market place. Traditional typesetters have declined sharply since the widespread use of computers which allow originators to send a disk (or even transmit copy down the telephone line) direct to printers.

Every business must in some sense be dependent. It is the degree of dependency that matters, along with the purchaser's perception of its risk. If your business is highly dependent, you will already be fully conversant with this type of risk as you will have been living under the Sword of Damocles, perhaps for many years.

Earn-out

In most circumstances you will get more money for your business if you are prepared to stay a while to ensure a smooth hand-over and to be paid (in part) at an agreed multiple of future profits. Nothing could seem simpler – but now part of the risk has been transferred to you. In nearly all earn-out situations some money will be paid on completion, but usually a substantial part is paid in the future – perhaps up to five years hence. All manner of awful things could happen during this time that will affect how much money you finally receive. You must evaluate the risk of more jam tomorrow against a smaller amount now.

A good corporate solicitor will as far as possible have a watertight agreement to protect your rights and allow you to maximise the earn-out payment. However, rarely is any thought given to what happens if, through ill-health or death, you cannot earn your money. A discussion with a good insurance broker is always worthwhile if you are considering accepting an earn-out.

No matter how legally watertight the earn-out agreement is, if the purchaser is unscrupulous and wants to ignore it there is little you can do but resort to litigation, where most victories are Pyrrhic. Your opponents will generally have more time and money than you, and will probably drag matters out to debilitate you financially. Choose your purchaser carefully.

The other major downside to earn-outs is what might happen if the acquirer goes bust. In such circumstances you could end up with nothing. It is possible, however, (although uncommon) to have a legal charge over the shares you have sold, so that you get them back if you don't receive all the money due to you.

For the above reasons, many people will not consider an earn-out except for a small part of the total price. In reality, however, the overwhelming majority of earn-outs do work properly.

The upside is that the acquirer may be prepared to pay considerably more on a deferred basis and you will have the opportunity to benefit from any additional growth he brings to the business.

Form of consideration

Subject to tax planning, there is no substitute for one hundred per cent cash on the table. However, as referred to in the previous section, most purchasers are less aggressive about price if there is an element of deferred consideration; for example, loan notes with deferred encashment dates. Also attractive to quoted companies is acceptance of their shares, which you agree to hold for a minimum period and which may have deferred dividend rights.

Again, you need to assess the risks against the rewards.

Industry norms

In some industries there are generally accepted methods of valuation. For example, in the security guard business it is common to value an acquisition as a percentage of turnover, a nursing home on the number of beds, and investment management companies on a percentage of funds under management. A few years ago, before their bubble burst, Body Shop franchises had a standard minimum price. The usual price factors as discussed in this chapter had only a small effect.

If the normal industry valuation produces a lower value than could otherwise be reasonably expected for a business in a different industry, it would be wise to approach buyers who are not in the industry and therefore not wedded to this form of valuation.

Interest rates

Other things being equal, the higher prevailing interest rates, the lower the value of a company, and vice versa. The theory is that extra profit is required from a business to match the higher return offered by putting the money on deposit (or the cost of borrowing the money to finance the purchase). In practice, interest rates have very little direct effect on valuations. This is because vendors will generally not accept a lower price simply on account of high interest rates and will if necessary wait a couple of years until there is a change in the economic cycle.

Management

Good quality management is always of value. From the purchaser's perspective, having continuity of good managers causes less disruption to the business in terms of customer and supplier relationships, and less apprehension with the staff. It makes the whole transaction less risky as the new owner has the benefit of their experience to fall back on. Good remaining management also gives the impression that what is being bought is a real business rather than an empire based on one man.

Obligations

The majority of obligations come in two forms: leases and employee costs. Where a business has commitments, it can (a) affect the ability of new owners to make changes and (b) create long-term demands on the business which have to be met even though they are no longer relevant to the current business.

Property leases (which only a decade ago were considered assets) can, in the current climate, be extremely difficult to dispose of. If the lease has "upwards only" rent reviews, the cost of moving premises could be huge. The current rent (at the inflated rate) will already have been taken into account in assessing current profits – but the sting in the tail is that to move, your business would, in one way or another, have to subsidise another business's occupation of your old premises for the duration of the lease. A lease can also represent a commitment under hire-purchase or lease-purchase agreements. Some capital equipment, such as a £1m printing press, create a very big commitment to fund each month.

Employee costs are not only the cost of terminating long-term contracts with senior executives. They are also the potential redundancy costs accruing to an ageing and long-standing workforce. In a sluggish manufacturing business, the redundancy costs of moving production to another town can be several times the amount paid for the whole company.

Other obligations can include minimum royalty payments for the purchase of a patent, or the granting of exclusive selling rights for a region or country.

Order book

The best time to sell is when the order book is full. This will give a lot of comfort to a potential purchaser. It is astounding how many otherwise logical, calculating businessmen react to a low order book by deciding to sell. And if you have already decided to sell, don't let the business run down before you do so. Work extra hard and attract orders, then if you still want to sell, fine. If you can't increase the order book, how can you expect anyone to pay a premium price for your business?

Price-Earnings ratios ("P/E")

There is a lot of nonsense talked about Price Earnings Ratios, especially in relation to private companies.

A P/E ratio is calculated by taking the latest reported post tax profits of a company and comparing them against the value of the company. In publicly quoted companies it is easy to calculate the P/E as the published accounts of a quoted company are required to show the amount of (post-tax) earnings per share. This gives you the "E" of the "P/E". The "P" is the price per share, and this can be easily ascertained from *The Financial Times,* other quality newspapers, etc. Many newspapers, including *The Financial Times,* show the P/E as well as the price of each share. In a private company the P/E is derived by dividing the value of the company (e.g. the offer from a purchaser) by the post-tax profit for the year. So a P/E of, say, ten means that the value of the company is equal to ten times last year's post-tax profits.

A quick glance down the share prices pages of *The Financial Times* shows that some companies have P/Es of six or seven whilst others are in the 70's and 80's. Why such a huge disparity? The reason is simple: the "E" is based on past results while the "P" is the current share price, reflecting anticipation of *future* earnings. High P/Es reflect an expectation of rapid profit growth; low P/Es reflect an assumption of stagnant or even declining profits.

Whilst P/Es can give a rough guide to the valuation levels applicable to different industry sectors, and different kinds of company within each sector, remember that in each specific case the P/E is affected daily by particular announcements or events relating to the company concerned. In any event the price investors will pay for a quoted investment where they can realise their investment at a moment's notice is obviously much higher than the price they might be prepared to pay for a share of an unlisted company.

There are many different kinds of P/E, in addition to the normal calculation referred to above, depending on the earnings figure used in the calculation: "prospective P/Es" relate price to anticipated future earnings; "fully diluted P/Es" adjust the earnings to allow for dilution if the company may have a commitment to issue some shares in the future or has done so part way through the previous year; "fully taxed P/Es" adjust the earnings to assume taxation at the normal rate if the company has benefited from a lower tax rate; "pre-tax P/Es" are calculated using pre-tax earnings as the name suggests. So, when in negotiations with prospective purchasers, and, having made sure which type of P/E you are dealing with you must also make sure that it is based on the appropriate "E"arnings. In many private businesses there is expenditure that would not be incurred if the purchaser owned it. This must be adjusted for.

For the most part, P/Es quoted for public companies give a fair approximation of that company's value although of course share prices often become volatile when a company is the subject of a takeover bid, or other speculation. In private companies it is a totally different ball game. The true profit a business is making is only really known to the vendor and the purchaser. Also, deals involving allegedly high P/Es for private companies are usually dependent on some earn-out and therefore at the time of the deal the actual P/E cannot be known by anyone. Add to this the boastful disposition of some vendors and the information disseminated via the traditional industry grapevine or trade press, and a totally misleading impression of company values is created.

The Financial Times gives a summary of the average P/Es of quoted companies for each industry sector. Probably the only relevance this has to sellers of private businesses is that private companies invariably sell at a significant discount to their quoted counterparts.

Potential

Potential is clearly a major influence on price. A growing company in a growing market is clearly worth more than a company with the same profits but which is declining in a declining industry. Potential could be there because of the growth that would occur from being part of a larger group – such as wider distribution, shared technological developments, and cost cutting. For each different type of purchaser a good intermediary will detail the additional benefits that would accrue from the acquisition. The purchaser will, of course, be fully aware of these benefits – it is for the intermediary to inform the purchaser that you also know them and that this must be reflected in the price.

Notwithstanding synergistic gains, the full inherent potential of the business must be demonstrated in the Information Memorandum. The most effective method of doing this is to include detailed profit and loss and cash flow projections (see page 41). This can mean a lot of work, especially if your business is not used to producing them, but even just the promise of "more jam tomorrow" can only have a positive effect on the selling price.

Profit history

If profits have been volatile in the past, there will obviously be concern that they may be volatile again in the future. Purchasers will inevitably discount the current and forecast profit levels if there is a hint that the profits are either not consistent or not maintainable.

Purchaser

Choosing the right customers is as important for a successful business as is choosing the right suppliers. Choosing the right purchaser is no different.

Quoted companies can issue shares to finance an acquisition. The shares can, by prior arrangement, be simultaneously sold to raise the cash to pay you. The prior arrangement is usually called a "vendor placing" and should in practice be invisible to you. A similar technique as far as you are concerned is called a "rights issue". The advantage for quoted companies in being able to issue shares for acquisitions is that, other things being equal, if a company has a higher P/E ratio than it is paying for the acquisition, and if this P/E continues to be applied to the combined earnings, there is an automatic uplift in the value of the whole company which benefits the shareholders (and the value of the directors' share options). In effect the market ascribes a value to the acquired business higher than the price actually paid. The bigger the difference in the P/E's between the buying and selling companies, then the bigger the increase in value to the acquirer's shareholders. It follows that when paying a premium for your business the purchaser's shareholders are still better off than by not doing a deal at all, providing the P/E paid is below theirs. Therefore if you are negotiating with a quoted company, it is easy to ascertain whether they can pay more by checking their P/E, which will be quoted daily in *The Financial Times*.

Acquisitive quoted companies can be on a treadmill of needing to make acquisitions to justify their high P/E ratio. This is fine for you, selling the business, so long as you don't have to take the highly rated shares and hold them until the steam inevitably runs out. A classic line from the Chairman is, "Look, I know we are only paying you this amount, but take our shares and in eighteen months' time they will be worth double – just look at our track record!" If you find yourself on the receiving end of this, then ask the Chairman to guarantee the arrangement personally. It will soon become evident whether he has as much faith in his company as he is asking you to have! Quoted companies sometimes "have" to make an acquisition to mask their own shortcomings. If they are aware that their results are going to be below market expectations – resulting in a significant fall in the share price and therefore the threat of a takeover (and the directors being ousted) – they need to "buy" profits with an acquisition. Taking shares in such a company is not advisable.

Where a purchaser is borrowing the money, you need to be circumspect. Firstly, the deal might not go through because he may not have the wherewithal to borrow the money; secondly, you may end up negotiating with the funders as well as the purchaser – all supposedly on the same side but with different criteria. This all takes a lot more time and money (not least in increased legal costs) and you will not get an over-generous deal because (a) the funders (particularly venture capital firms) will not allow an excessive price to be paid no matter how keen the front man is, and (b) interest will have to be paid on the borrowed money putting an additional strain on profits and cash flows.

Having said that, many deals are done using borrowings to finance them, but a decisive, financially able purchaser will generally mean a smooth progression to a satisfactory deal for both sides and can save substantially on your legal costs.

The third aspect to choosing the right purchaser, as alluded to elsewhere in this book, is that of finding one who can add substantially to the value of your company, perhaps by cutting out several hundred thousand pounds in costs which are duplicated in his business – such as the accounts department, premises, or the sales director. A purchaser will not pay you for all the added value he will generate, but he may share some of it with you as it is in his interest to do the deal.

Quality of earnings

If Company A makes the same profit each year as Company B, it might seem logical to assume that the companies have the same value. This ignores the "quality" of those profits. If company A has five-year cleaning contracts with (say) government departments, then a prospective purchaser knows that the company he is buying has a secure future. Without taking on any new business, it will survive in the short term, is not readily open to predatory attacks from the competition and is not dependent on key staff staying with the company. Company B, on the other hand, is a graphic design company whose order book is never more than four weeks' sales. Customers may be fickle, going elsewhere without warning. If one or two key staff left (or lost their creative thrust) they would be difficult to replace and even more difficult to go into competition with. In this scenario, would you be prepared to pay the same for each company?

Quality of earnings is also linked to dependency (see page 50).

Quality of earnings is really a comfort factor for purchasers. The effect, though, is very real. This is why, traditionally, quoted property companies have on average, a higher P/E ratio than builders' merchants.

Size

Generally, the larger and more established a business is, the higher its P/E ratio. This is simply because the business is less vulnerable to attack; it will have a better infrastructure, and is therefore safer. It is also true that it is easier to raise £10m of funding for an acquisition than it is to raise £250k for equally viable propositions.

There is, strangely, a psychological aspect to pricing. Typically in manufacturing businesses, no matter how good the profits are, buyers will rarely pay more than the turnover for a business.

Whilst many of the above factors are obvious, and some overlap, it does not necessarily follow that the absence of certain advantages will deter all purchasers or affect the price. For example, it could be that a purchaser wants to capitalise on your distribution network but close down your factory and move production to his own works – in this case he would be delighted if there were no senior management staying on, who would be expensive to dismiss.

The purchaser interested in the rum-tot vessels company

might have (as his hidden agenda) the plan to shift production to giftwares, and therefore the only effect the Royal Navy dependency has is on the price negotiations with you. The moral of this story is that if your business has a "downside", it does not have to affect the price unless you let it.

It is always surprising to see how much a purchaser will pay for a business he really wants.

6

Vendor Politics

If you live long enough, you will see everything.

"Vendor politics" is a horrible piece of jargon. It means that the vendor has got his act together and is prepared to negotiate seriously for the sale of his business. What could be simpler? You want to sell and someone else wants to buy. However, the reality can be so different. The purchaser is about to spend a considerable sum on accountancy, due diligence, legal fees (it is the purchaser's solicitor who prepares the Sale and Purchase Agreement), tax advice and the opportunity cost of working on the acquisition of your business. Therefore, before doing so the purchaser will make sure that the vendor really does want to sell and that negotiations can be undertaken in a timely and professional manner. If a purchaser is not convinced of your determination to conclude a deal, he may well decide that he should pursue other opportunities, or he may ask you to indemnify him for his professional costs. In the former instance you may have lost the opportunity of getting the best deal; in the latter instance you may be happy to proceed on this basis, but if something totally outside your control happens before you and he have signed on the bottom line – his solicitor may find a fault in your title to the freehold premises; you have a major fire in your warehouse; you have a heart-attack – then you will have to pick up the bill for his professional fees at a time when you need extra expenses like you need a hole in the head. These extra costs are unlikely to be allowed against tax, and you will certainly not be able to recover the VAT.

Having a professional intermediary who is fully prepared shows that you are serious about selling. It also gives the purchaser a degree of comfort that negotiations are unlikely to founder because of an unforeseen technicality. Thirdly, and perhaps most significantly, it enables you to take a tough line without being confrontational – this is of particular importance if you will continue to work in the business under the new ownership, either for transitional purposes or perhaps as part of an earn-out arrangement.

It is possible to have detailed negotiations running with two or more interested parties. At first glance, this may appear an attractive method of keeping your options open and thereby securing the best price. If you do try and keep too many balls in the air there is a fair to middling chance you will drop them all. The reality is that if you are running with several prospective purchasers it probably means that you are not at all convinced that you will actually conclude a deal with any of them. There is also the waste of an amazing amount of management time and resource that is needed to have detailed negotiations with several interested purchasers. It is probably better that you stop dealing with all of them and find a really suitable purchaser – this of course may mean that you change your advisers.

Apart from all this there are real commercial concerns about divulging extremely confidential information and giving access to key staff to several purchasers, some of whom may be competitors. What happens to the value of your business if negotiations break down or you proceed with someone else and detailed information about your business is then commonly known? Should one of the parties become aware that you are in detailed negotiations with someone else they may perceive that you have been acting in bad faith in allowing them to incur substantial professional costs without informing them of the possible risk that you will sell to someone else. This may well cause them to act in bad faith towards your business and "unfairly" use the information they have gleaned.

From a practical point of view, once basic terms have been agreed, a purchaser will invariably want a lock-out or exclusivity period. It is of course down to you to decide if that is what you want but if it is not raised then you should be wary about the ability of the purchaser and his professional advisers.

Moving to the tactical aspects of negotiation, there are many ways to deal with potential purchasers. It is for you to decide what is right for you in your circumstances.

On price, one ploy is not to meet anyone until they have submitted an indicative offer price, based on the Information Memorandum, for your consideration. This way you will (a) avoid wasting time meeting purchasers who would not have met your price expectations, and (b) have a "ball park" figure on which to negotiate. This technique can work, but it eliminates purchasers who do not want to commit themselves to price at such an early stage. It also lends itself very well to the negotiation technique of "offer the seller what he wants, then as new facts come to light (as they invariably do during due diligence investigations, etc.) take things away from the offer until you end up paying what you want". This approach is used widely, though surreptitiously and with cunning.

In any event, allow potential purchasers to visit your premises only the minimum number of times. This implies to a potential purchaser that there are several others negotiating to buy the business, and stops him gleaning further confidential information when he may not in the end be the actual purchaser. Also, strangers have a very disturbing effect on staff, and there are no guarantees that a potential purchaser will become the actual purchaser.

When negotiating on price, there is a golden rule: "He who speaks first loses". Break this rule at your financial peril. You cannot possibly know what the potential purchaser wants to do with your business and therefore how much he is prepared to pay. Be laid back when talking of price – he must make the first move. Beyond this small piece of advice, it would take another whole book on the art of negotiating to impart anything else that is so important.

You should be aware that most of the concessions that you will make (even on price) occur in the presence of solicitors during the long and laborious discussions over the Sale and Purchase Agreement (see chapter 8). So be on your guard. You will have great difficulty winning every negotiation point – just make sure you win the important ones. Never forget why you are selling and what you want to achieve.

From a negotiating stance, your absence during the detailed negotiations is very effective, providing you are not concerned if one particular buyer withdraws from the deal. By being absent, perhaps abroad (see "Taxation", page 69), you stop any of the coercion that usually occurs after several hours around a lawyer's conference room table, with each side trying to complete a deal. Indeed, using this trick, the purchasers will often give way to your nominated representative on a particular point at issue in order to progress matters as they know that he will have to contact you for instructions (which can take several days) unless they relent. This approach may lead to slightly higher legal costs, but it does prevent you from being manipulated during the lengthy negotiations over the Sale and Purchase Agreement and allow you time to reflect on the bigger issues. It also allows you to stonewall on an issue without their having any means of appeal – therefore if they really want to do the deal, they will give in.

If you have a minimum price below which you will not sell, and the potential purchaser wants to negotiate on that price, do not be drawn into trying to justify it. You will be open to attack on the basis of your calculations, and are bound to be the loser.

You have nothing to gain by having to justify the price you want. It is for the potential purchaser to try to justify to himself that the price is acceptable. If he can do this, he will pay; if he can't do it, he won't pay – it's as simple as that.

You can sometimes feel unsure of a potential purchaser. His offer may be the highest, or the most suitable for what you are trying to achieve, but you may have doubts about his seriousness, or about his financial ability. An acid test is to ask him to indemnify you against (reasonable) legal costs should he withdraw from the transaction. He may ask you to reciprocate, and indemnify him should you withdraw, but at least you will be more comfortable in incurring legal costs if you have security that the potential purchaser is acting in good faith.

Should you have meetings at the purchaser's premises, do not sign the visitors' book. All nosy salesmen read them when signing in, so this would be tantamount to an announcement to the industry that you were "in talks" about selling your business. Similarly, when you have potential purchasers known within the industry visiting your premises, remove the signing-in book.

Once the terms have been agreed, professional advisers like having Heads of Agreement prepared before proceeding to either due diligence or the Sale and Purchase Agreement. The advantages are that the Heads of Agreement set out in simple outline what has been agreed between you and the purchaser, and thus should avoid any misunderstanding between the parties. The Heads of Agreement also act as the starting point for briefing each party's lawyers. All this is true, but in practice the actual deal often bears little resemblance to the Heads of Agreement, which can require considerable extra up-front work. Do not be misled into believing that the Heads of Agreement are always binding, even if they explicitly state that they are and everyone signs as such. In reality, so much changes on both sides that it can be impossible to sue on the original document, even if it has been drafted by solicitors.

Sample Heads of Agreement are shown in Appendix V.

7

Taxation

It's not what you earn – it's how much you keep.

The good news is that all taxation on the sale of a business is voluntary! If you really don't want to pay tax on the sale proceeds, then you don't have to. Some tax planning may of course be necessary, and some of the inconvenience may not be considered to be worthwhile – even to save £1,000,000.

By far the simplest method of saving tax is to emigrate. This may not be as drastic as it first appears. After a life of hard work, what could be difficult about living in the South of France, or even Jersey? You would need to leave the UK before you decided to enter into an agreement to sell your business, and before 6 April in the tax year in which you actually sell it. You may also have to sell your home so that you don't have a place of residence in the UK and be able to demonstrate that you really are centered abroad.. By emigrating you are not banished from the UK. You can return to the UK for limited periods (in theory, up to 180 days per year! but no more than 90 on average) and you can even return permanently but only after a sufficient lapse of time, but with substantially enhanced wealth. The standard time that you are required not to be resident in the UK is five full tax years. There are however several loopholes whereby the absence can be reduced to one full tax year.

If short-term emigration is not for you, then another way to save tax is to sell your company for shares or loan stock in the acquiring company. Tax is payable only when the shares are finally sold or the loan stock encashed (this can be piecemeal, and you can utilise the annual capital gains tax exemption – currently in excess of £10,000). If you hold them until your death, they will totally escape capital gains tax. They will form part of your estate for inheritance tax – but so would the cash, on which you would also already have paid capital gains tax. It can be risky to take shares in any company, and to have virtually your entire wealth locked into one company is a very high-risk strategy. If financial security is not high on your agenda, you don't need the ready cash and you are impressed with how good a deal the management of the acquiring company did with you, then consider taking shares. If you are worried about security, loan notes may be safer but you should consider whether they can be secured, or preferably guaranteed by a bank. Interest could be paid to you quarterly or half-yearly, and the notes could be secured against the acquiring company's assets so that, if things do go wrong, you get your money before anyone else, even before H.M. Customs & Revenue. If all you intend to do with your sale proceeds is "stick it in the building society", then this route can give you a pre-agreed rate of interest, and this is calculated on the gross sale proceeds rather than on the after-tax sale proceeds you would have in the building society. The rate of interest itself would probably also be higher, reflecting the acquirer's marginal cost of capital (and, if held until death, also avoids capital gains tax). Purchasers, too, are often attracted to these methods of paying for acquisitions, as there is no immediate outflow of cash. They may therefore be prepared to pay you more for your business.

Still not happy? Then, within three years, roll over the taxable capital gain part of the proceeds (not necessarily the whole proceeds) into ordinary shares in an unquoted trading company. There are certain restrictions on the types of trade that can be undertaken (these are listed in Appendix VII), but it could still be a fairly passive business activity to keep you mildly occupied during retirement. It could be a company belonging to an old friend in which you effectively become partners, or you could set your son or daughter up in business. In addition, if you, your family or current business partners control less than 30% of the shares, the first £500,000 of investment should be eligible for Enterprise Investment Scheme relief which incredibly produces a negative tax rate of 20% – you actually get a rebate from the Inland Revenue. If none of the above is suitable and you do prefer to pay tax, all is not lost.

Entrepreneurs Relief was introduced in the 2008 Budget. It has since had minor amendments but the upshot is that we now have the most benign tax regime on the sale of a family company since Capital Gains Tax was introduced in 1965.

Basically, each individual who sells more than 5% of the shares (or other business assets) in a private trading company is allowed the first £5m of gain to be taxed at 10%. This is an amount that most sellers of businesses are happy to pay. Above this and after the annual exemption, higher rate tax payers will suffer 28% tax. Married couples have a combined £10m of gain at 10% – a great tax planning opportunity! The shares need to have been held for at least one year and each spouse must be a director or employee of the company, so some planning may be necessary. The £5m is a lifetime limit so serial entrepreneurs need to be careful but crystallised gains made prior to 6th April 2008 are excluded..

Undoubtedly the biggest "elephant trap" to be aware of is having a surplus of non-business assets within your business. Non-business assets could be investment property, stocks and shares or it could be cash. Too much of any of these may prevent eligibility for Entrepreneurs Relief.

Several wily businessmen who have heard of Entrepreneurs Relief and the 10% tax rate have stopped paying themselves dividends which attract higher rate income tax and therefore built-up a healthy cash surplus in their company, then decided to sell only to be advised that because of the cash in the company it is not eligible for Entrepreneurs Relief. Unfortunately there is no prior clearance procedure available from the taxman so if you do get it wrong then you will pay the 28% capital gains tax. You have been warned!

There is another trap you need to be wary of if you are selling the business on an earn-out, have a contract of employment during the earn-out period and if you leave during the earn-out period and lose your entitlement to the earn-out. This arrangement is common in "people businesses" such as advertising and recruitment. With such an arrangement the Inland Revenue may seek to tax the earn-out as income from employment (and therefore taxable at up to 50% plus national insurance contributions) and not as a capital gain!

The 2002 Budget introduced a relief whereby when a company sells a substantial shareholding in a subsidiary then any gain is free of tax. Whilst this is a very welcome relief for large trading groups, it is unlikely to produce much benefit for owner-managers who wish to sell their entire business and retire. Firstly, both the holding company and the subsidiary being sold immediately before and after the sale must be trading companies: so there must be at least two "trading activities" in current ownership. Secondly, if the holding company is then sold it is unlikely that Entrepreneurs Relief would be available as the holding company would then be likely to have surplus cash within it.

On another tack, pre-sale pension contributions can also be used as a tax-free way to acquire some benefits for you and your spouse.

All of the above are simple outlines of tax-saving

opportunities. They are examples of only some of the things that can be achieved to maximise your return for the years of hard work (and family suffering!) that have gone into building your business. Although it is a long established tenet of English law that a person may organise their affairs to minimise tax, it is also well established that artificial transactions solely for the purpose of reducing tax are ineffective. As with all tax advice, planning needs to be considered alongside your specific circumstances, and professional advice must be sought before taking any action.

It is also important to realise that these tax saving opportunities will not exist forever. It is very dangerous to plan for the future using the tax laws as they are now.

Should you for whatever reason decide to pay capital gains tax, it becomes due for payment on the 31 January following the 5 April after the deal (and for tax purposes, the deal is treated as being the date of formally entering the agreement – not the date when you get the money) so, if negotiations are taking place in February or March, it is as well to consider actually signing the agreement after 5 April.

8

The Sale and Purchase Agreement

*The main purpose of English law is to make more
work for itself.*

The Sale and Purchase Agreement is a horrendous document.
It is probably the most important piece of paper you will ever
sign, and yet there will be large parts that you won't
understand. It is full of awful jargon, and some of the phrases,
in Latin as well as English, you will never come across again
and will probably never want to.

So it will come to pass that your solicitor and their solicitor
will want you to sign and take responsibility for a document
half an inch thick and on which, to a great extent, your future
prosperity depends.

Some businessmen take the approach, "I trust my solicitor,
but if anything does go wrong I can always sue him". This
attitude can seem to work because things do not usually go
wrong, but if they do and you want to sue your solicitor over a
document you yourself signed (and you now haven't got any
money anyway) – forget it. It is far better to understand what
the risks are in the first place and to make your own assessment.

For insomniacs and serious sellers, an example of a Sale and Purchase Agreement is included as Appendix V. This example is not definitive. There are so many variations on how an acquisition can be structured that no one example could cover every situation.

In theory, everything in a Sale and Purchase Agreement is "by agreement", and therefore negotiable. In practice, if you did try to negotiate everything the result would probably be legal costs greater than the price you are getting for your business.

Solicitors are professionals. For their own satisfaction and edification (as well as to keep their professional indemnity insurance down), they will want to do a good job for you – at any price! Well-intentioned solicitors frequently argue at length over obscure clauses in the Sale and Purchase Agreement, trying to protect their respective clients. You and the purchaser should be aware of this highly remunerative tendency and be prepared to intervene.

The principle behind the Sale and Purchase Agreement is straightforward: it details who is buying what from whom, for how much and when. What could be simpler? It is not even necessary to have a written agreement. Some acquisitions occur simply by the vendor handing over a signed share transfer form and his share certificates in exchange for a cheque. This method of executing the transaction does, however, leave the purchaser exposed, so the purchaser's solicitor will want safeguards for his client and want them documented. For this reason it is the purchaser's solicitor who usually prepares the Sale and Purchase Agreement. And, as you will not know whether any of the safeguards being requested in the incomprehensible (draft) document are reasonable, you will have to consult a solicitor. What may have started out as a simple deal – in essence no different from the types of deal you have done all your business life – transmogrifies into an expensive, intellectually esoteric bun fight between two highly paid solicitors. Instead of being in control of your destiny, without realising it you find yourself being led round and round the mulberry bush and told what you must and must not do. You have been warned.

Do consider agreeing a fixed fee with your solicitor before he is appointed. He or she will not like it, but it will help procure an expedient transaction.

Sale and Purchase Agreements with quoted companies tend to be lengthier, as the purchase may be subject to obtaining shareholder approval at a specially convened meeting or, even more complicated, subject to a successful placing of shares to pay for the acquisition. Usually, both of these requirements are formalities – but they are formalities which have to be fully documented.

Obviously, the Sale and Purchase Agreement should be a record of the agreement you have with the purchaser. The initial agreement between the two parties will be refined and modified by the time an engrossed Sale and Purchase Agreement is produced. You must never lose sight of the basic terms of the agreement, and the fact that they are indeed recorded in the Sale and Purchase Agreement. This may seem trite, but after many days of many hours in a solicitor's office it can be very easy to lose sight of the wood for the trees.

Of the other points in the Sale and Purchase Agreement:

Interpretation

This section tries to explain the definition of terms that appear in the rest of the Agreement. Many of the definitions are obvious (e.g. Purchaser's Solicitors), but be careful: whenever any of the defined terms are used in the document, they mean the precise wording attributed to them and not what they may mean in normal usage

Do not be overly concerned about references to various sections of Taxes Acts or Companies Acts; this is an area you can leave to your solicitor.

Warranties and Disclosure Letter

The concept of giving warranties is very simple: you are explicitly guaranteeing certain facts about your business. Warranties apportion financial risk away from the purchaser (*caveat emptor*) to the seller. They are therefore safeguards for the Purchaser.

However, the warranties in the Sale and Purchase Agreement, which are drawn up by the purchaser's solicitor, will contain statements about your business that you have never made, or indeed that may not be true. It is your responsibility to go through each warranty, with your solicitor, and if it is not accurate state the correct position in a Disclosure Letter. This, therefore, is a very important document. It is your safeguard that there are no repercussions on you if, in the future, there are problems with the company concerning the information in the warranties.

The warranties are the basis of the safeguards the purchaser's solicitor uses to protect his client. Each individual warranty is there for a reason; fail to understand any of them at your peril.

It is a matter for negotiation as to which warranties you will or will not accept and what your Disclosure Letter may contain. In many instances the warranties are used to "flush out" any bad news about the company before the legally binding contract is signed. It can occur that a matter (say, specific litigation) is known of by both sides, but the purchasers do not allow it to be formally disclosed so that if it does cause loss to the company, then the amount of that loss will be down to you.

There is usually a minimum aggregate amount (which can vary from £1000 upwards) below which any loss to the company will not be recovered from you. There is also usually a maximum that can be recovered, which is very rarely greater than the price the purchaser is paying.

It is worth noting that over sixty per cent of a Sale and Purchase Agreement is usually devoted to warranties and indemnities.

Indemnities

Some matters are better dealt with as warranties, others as indemnities. Generally, warranties shift the responsibility for any loss to the company on to the vendor. The redress for such loss is usually damages awarded by a Court. To claim under a warranty the common law imposes a duty to establish and assess the loss and for such losses to be mitigated (i.e. to take all steps necessary to reduce the amount of the loss). Indemnities, however, shift responsibility purely and simply on a pound-for-pound basis, without the need to mitigate the loss. If a certain events happens (such as litigation from a former employee) you pay; there is no discussion. Indemnities are much more effective at parting you from your money.

Earn-outs

If your deal contains an earn-out provision do make sure that the wording of the appropriate clauses will work in practice. You know how your business works and what can affect it – your solicitor does not.

Earn-outs vary in length from a couple of months (to the end of the current financial year) to several years. For tax as well as commercial reasons the purchaser will want a limit on the maximum amount payable to you under the earn-out, so do not limit your potential upside by being too realistic if you are ever asked early in discussions what is the maximum profit the business could achieve in the next couple of years.

If the acquirer is a quoted company they will need to show continual improving profits so it may be possible to obtain an undertaking in the Sale and Purchase Agreement that they will do what they can to improve the profitability of the business during the earn-out period.

There are generally two ways to protect the future profits of the business you have sold so that you can maximise your earn-out. The simplest way is that you are allowed, unfettered, to manage the business for the period of the earn-out. Any dealings with the new owner (or associated companies) will be solely at your discretion. Whilst this can be appropriate it may hinder the reasons why the purchaser wants the business. The other method is whereby the purchaser runs the business but you have the ability to veto anything they do. In reality it does not stop them from doing what they want but the effects of such actions will be "added back" in the earn-out calculation.

In any case, it is always better for your auditors to continue in office until the expiration of the earn-out period and for them to do the calculation of the earn-out rather than the acquirer's auditors.

Completion

The completion section sets out what each party to the transaction has to do at the "completion meeting" in order for you to receive your banker's draft. If any of the requirements are not met it can scupper the deal. In complex transactions, rehearsal completion meetings are held to try to eliminate last-minute hitches.

At the completion meeting, the Sale and Purchase Agreement and stock transfer forms are signed. There are usually a series of directors' and shareholders' meetings involving resignation and appointment of directors, company secretary, auditors, change of registered office, bank mandates and possibly a new Memorandum and Articles of Association. Fortunately, all this is orchestrated by the solicitors.

Restrictive covenants

Depending on the nature of the deal, it is usual for the vendors to agree that they will not compete against their old company for a specific period of time – often three to five years. The restrictions may have geographical limitations, and include current customers and even the poaching of staff. So do not think that you will get a large slug of money to fund you setting-up in direct competition.

Restrictive covenants are a continually changing area of the law so your solicitor will not be able to give you absolute advice but generally speaking the tougher the restrictions are the better it is for you: they are more likely to be unenforceable.

9

How to Live Happily Ever After

Let MacIntyre Hudson look after all your financial needs

You've sold the business and can finally realise your dreams: the yacht, the sports car, possibly that little Caribbean island you've always longed for. Having done the hard work, surely spending your money will be simple?

Sadly, things are never that straightforward. Effective planning will prove just as important to you now as it was during your working years. Professional wealth promotion and retention advice is crucial in ensuring you can continue to enjoy the fruits of your labour long into the future.

MacIntyre Hudson, chartered accountants and business advisers, provide a comprehensive range of services for high net worth individuals. We advise on all aspects of UK and international tax compliance, tax planning and wealth management. We can help whether you're looking to maximise the benefits of your tax status or considering the tax and financial implications of a specific activity, such as:

- **Setting up a new business** – Whether you are setting up a new business or reinvesting your wealth in another business, we can advise on all aspects of business formation, from business incorporation to advice on VAT structures, employee benefits, share schemes, pensions and expatriate tax.

- **Investing your nest-egg** – We provide a range of holistic and integrated services, from investment portfolio management and benchmarking analysis to financial planning and analysis review. We also offer all our clients a free review with the experienced Independent Financial Advisers of Carrwood MacIntyre who we have worked with for many years.

- **Investing in assets in the UK and abroad** – whether overseas properties, art, yachts or private businesses – from start-ups to established entities.

- **Estate planning** – We can help protect and maximise your wealth by establishing and administering trusts, wills and estates. Effective estate planning ensures your assets are protected, wealth passed on as you wish and tax minimised.

- **Moving overseas** – We help manage cross-border tax issues and requirements, both at home and abroad. Our services are extended overseas via our membership of Morison International, a global association of independent accountants, auditors, tax advisers, business consultants and lawyers. So no matter where you are in the world. we will ensure that you get the best possible commercial and tax efficient advice.

- **Charitable giving** – If you want to give something back to the community, we can advise you as a trustee or set up and advise on charities.

- **Responding to a tax investigation** – We can help in the eventuality of a tax enquiry or investigation, whether a voluntary disclosure, HMRC or serious fraud investigation.

Whatever your plans, MacIntyre Hudson can provide the professional advice you need to plan for the future.

The MacIntyre Hudson personal touch

MacIntyre Hudson is one of the UK's largest accounting firms. Yet, we provide the partner led, personal attention that clients expect.

This personal touch is backed by experience and specialists. In addition to individuals, we provide audit, tax and advisory services for owner-managed and entrepreneurial businesses, as well as some of the top listed businesses across a number of industry sectors in the UK, Europe and internationally.

We take time to understand each client's ambitions and priorities, tailoring what we do to suit them. We see the obstacles and opportunities and share their vision. We truly believe that the future is what you make it and that our approach makes a long-term difference to our clients' success.

Carrwood MacIntyre Financial Planning

Carrwood MacIntyre is an Independent Financial Advisers who provide MacIntyre Hudson's private clients, owner-managers, multi-national employers and trustees of private, family, charitable and pension trusts with much more than investment advice

Their range of investment services have been designed to provide the right investment solution to meet a client's personal circumstances and requirements. They take your whole financial situation into account in order to develop a complete approach to the management and growth of your wealth – for you, your family, future generations, as well as your business.

MacIntyre Hudson Private Client Services

As we go through life, our personal circumstances change and different tax implications affect our personal funds. Not to mention, many of us don't have time for record keeping or feel daunted by the magnitude of tax information.

MacIntyre Hudson' personal tax advisers have established long-lasting relationships with our clients. We treat our private clients' needs with the same urgency as those of large companies and provide individually-tailored services.

Our team is accessible, approachable, and doesn't hide behind complicated tax jargon and financial lingo.

We do more than file and review tax returns. We proactively help clients plan their financial path through life with the aim of achieving their business and personal goals, and even take on the role of counsellor through life's more challenging milestones.

For more information visit www.macintyrehudson.co.uk

Appendix I

Checklist of Information Required to Prepare an Information Memorandum

Accounts

- Statutory accounts and detailed profit and loss accounts for each of the last five financial years, plus explanation of any exceptional or extraordinary matters for the company and each of its subsidiaries

- For each of the last five years, details of any income or expenditure not directly related to trading, e.g. wives' cars charged to the business, excessive pension contributions, etc.

- Latest management accounts

- Any budgets and cash flow projections prepared for the business (see Chapter 4)

Sales

- Details of any customer who accounts for more than five per cent of the turnover in the current and previous financial years

- Copies of any sales/agency agreements with third parties

- Copies of all promotion material, including advertisements

- Copy of the aged debtors' listing

Purchases

- Details of any supplier who accounts for more than ten per cent of purchases in the current and previous financial years

- Copies of any supplier agreements

- Copy of the aged creditors' report

Production

- A description of each of the processes, and in particular any distinguishing abilities of the business

- A listing of major items of plant and equipment with the date of acquisition, original cost, net book value, current market value and replacement cost

- An analysis of turnover for the current and previous financial years between:

    - Bought-in components
    - Manufactured components
    - Bought-in complete products

Directors and staff

- An organisation chart, including names and job titles

- For directors, executives and key personnel, a schedule of names, ages, job descriptions, lengths of service, salaries and any benefits, including cars and pensions

- Details of those who would be leaving the company on a change of ownership

- A brief career resume for each director and senior executive

- Details of any long-term Consultants

Assets

- Details of freehold properties and current market valuations

- Details of leasehold properties and copies of the leases

- Details of trademarks, trade names, copyrights or other intellectual property of the company or its subsidiaries

- Details of investments

- Details of any assets or liabilities which may not form part of the Sale

Sundry

- A copy of the bank facility letter

- Details of pension commitments

- Details of any onerous or other agreements not made in the ordinary course of business

- Details of awards or membership of associations

Appendix II

Good Business Limited

Information Memorandum (sample)

Contents

Disclaimer
1. Background and History
2. Sales
3. Operations
4. Management and Staff
5. Financial

Appendices
I   Organisation Chart
II   Major Items of Plant & Equipment
III Market Sector Activities
IV   Audited Accounts for the Year Ended 30th April 2010
V   Financial Projections for the Three Years Ending 30th April 2013
VI   ISO 9002 Certificate
VII Promotional Literature

Disclaimer

The purpose of this Information Memorandum is to assist the recipient in deciding whether to investigate the possibility of acquiring Good Business Limited ("Good Business"). The Information Memorandum is not intended to form the basis of any acquisition decision. Each recipient must make its own independent assessment in order to determine its interest in acquiring Good Business and should obtain independent professional advice.

The information in this Information Memorandum has been supplied by the management of Good Business and has not been independently verified by MacIntyre Hudson Corporate Finance Ltd. Neither MacIntyre Hudson Corporate Finance Ltd nor Good Business nor any of their respective officers, agents or employees give or have any authority to give any representation or warranty (express or implied) for the accuracy and completeness of this Information Memorandum or any other written or oral communication transmitted or made available to a prospective purchaser, nor shall they be liable in any way for any inaccuracy, omission or misleading statement herein. Only those particular formal representations which may be made to the purchaser in a formal agreement as and when it is finally executed, and subject to such limitations and restrictions as may be specified therein, shall have any legal effect.

This Information Memorandum has been delivered to interested parties for information purposes only and upon the express understanding that such parties will use it for the purposes set out above. In furnishing this Information Memorandum, MacIntyre Hudson Corporate Finance Ltd and Good Business undertake no obligation to provide the recipient with access to any additional information or to update this Information Memorandum or to correct any inaccuracies therein which may become apparent and reserve the right, without advance notice, to change the procedure for the acquisition or to terminate negotiations at any time prior to the signing of any binding agreement for the acquisition. In no circumstances will MacIntyre Hudson Corporate Finance Ltd or Good Business be responsible for any costs or expenses incurred in connection with any preparation and submission of preliminary purchase proposals or for any other costs and expenses incurred by potential purchasers in connection with the proposed acquisition.

All enquiries and communications of whatever nature regarding the proposed sale should be directed only to Gary Morley at the following address:-

> MacIntyre Hudson Corporate Finance Ltd
> New Bridge Street House
> 30-34 New Bridge Street
> London EC4V 6BJ
>
> Tel: +44 (0)20 7429 4100
> Mob: +44 (0)7973 334391
> Email: Gary.Morley@mhllp.co.uk

Under no circumstances should prospective purchasers make contact with the owners, management, employees, customers, suppliers or other professional advisers of the business until invited to do so by MacIntyre Hudson Corporate Finance Ltd.

1. Background and History

1.1   Good Business Limited is a highly successful manufacturer and distributor of shu-shu valves to the film production industry. Currently approximately half of the company's sales are from their own production. The balance are imported.

1.2   Good Business was founded in Coventry in 1948 by Sydney James. It was acquired in 1978 by the current owner and managing director, Jim Dale.

1.3   The business moved to the present 20,000 sq.ft. site in Leicester in 1992.

1.4   Jim Dale with his wife are the only directors of the company. Mrs. Dale is not involved with the management of the company.

1.5   The current shareholdings are:-

Jim Dale	78%
Mrs. Dale	18%
Barbara Windsor (Mr. Dale's sister)	4%
	100%

1.6   Mr. Dale is now 69 and wishes to retire. The whole of the shares in the company are offered for sale.

1.7   Mr. Dale would be happy to remain with the company for an agreed period to ensure a smooth handover to a new owner.

1.8   It is anticipated that the recent favourable tax breaks available to films produced in the UK will have a favourable effect on the company's business.

2. Sales

2.1   Shu-shu valves are consumable products used in the film production business. They are sold both direct to film production companies and also to film equipment hire companies for re-sale. All of the company's sales are in the UK.

2.2　An example of the company's promotional literature is attached as Appendix VII.

2.3　Approximately one-third of sales are direct to film production companies. The selling price to the hire companies is approximately 25% lower than for direct sales.

2.4　Approximately 3% of total sales are returned from the film production companies for full credit. There is no such return policy for the film equipment hire companies.

2.5　The company has approximately sixty film equipment hire companies as customers. This is approximately one-third of the market.

2.6　None of the film equipment hire companies accounts for more than 5% of the company's sales.

2.7　The average order value is approximately £10,000.

2.8　An analysis of market sector activities is shown in Appendix III.

2.9　The company employs a sales manager and a salesman, both of whom spend substantially the whole amount of their time out of the office.

2.10　The sales manager; Kenneth Williams (age 48), has been with the company for ten years. The salesman; Charles Hawtrey (age 31), has been with the company for three years.

2.11　There is a certain amount of technical input needed for each sale. The salesman advises on the best type of shu-shu valve required and approximate quantity needed depending on the type of film production e.g. comedy, action, erotic, musical.

2.12 The company advertises extensively in trade magazines as well as sponsoring several technical awards at national industry events.

2.13 Good Business is the only UK based manufacturer of shu-shu valves, the competition being mainly US manufacturers who import direct to the film equipment hire companies.

3.   Operations

3.1   The company operates from one site in Leicester.

3.2   The general manager; Frankie Howerd (age 51), has direct responsibility for buying, production and stock control.

3.3   The company manufactures the two most commonly used types of shu-shu valve: in line and polarised.

3.4   The flanges and balls are machined and tooled in house. The plastic bearings and cowlings manufacturing is sub-contracted. All assembly is carried out on site.

3.5   The company employs eight tongue and groovers and has five apprentices.

3.6   The premises are split approximately:-

Office accommodation	7,000 sq.ft.
Warehousing and distribution	5,000 sq.ft.
Manufacturing and assembly	8,000 sq.ft.
	20,000 sq.ft.

3.7   There is a sophisticated computerised stock control/production management system which integrates into the company's management information system and financial accounts.

3.8   Orders are received approximately three months ahead of delivery, enabling the company to have a relatively low stockholding requirement.

3.9 The company is ISO 9002 registered.

3.10 A list of major items of plant and equipment is attached as Appendix II.

4. Management and Staff

4.1 Attached as Appendix I is the organisation chart of the company. The company currently employs 41 staff.

4.2 Jim Dale is the chairman of the company. Since 2007 he has worked three days a week.

4.3 There is a management committee which comprises:-

Sales Manager	Charles Hawtrey
General Manager	Frankie Howerd
Administration Manager	Hattie Jacques

Apart from strategic decisions, all day to day operations of the business are decided upon by the management committee which meets weekly.

4.4 Ms. Jacques, when required, also acts as Mr. Dale's personal assistant.

4.5 The accounts department, which consists of a purchase ledger clerk, a sales ledger clerk and a part-time payroll clerk, all report to Hattie Jacques.

4.6 Apart from the directors, there is no pension scheme. Mr. Dale's remuneration package reflects his ownership of the company.

5. Financial

5.1 Attached as Appendix IV are the audited accounts for the year ended 30th April 2010.

5.2 Attached as Appendix V are the financial projections for the three years ending 30th April 2013.

5.3 Summary

£'000	Actual			Forecast		
	2008	2009	2010	2011	2012	2013
Sales	3,384	3,678	3,965	4,201	4,453	4,717
Gross profit	900	990	1,135	1,288	1,399	1,504
Gross margin	26.6%	26.9%	28.6%	30.7%	31.4%	31.9%
Overheads	566	598	633	686	751	816
Operating profit	334	392	502	602	648	688
Mr. Dales's costs inc. in the above	130	137	140	156	158	165
Interest	(44)	(23)	(9)	4	18	31
Restated profit before tax	420	506	633	762	824	884

5.4   All expenditure on research and development is written off in the year it is incurred.

5.5   The freehold of the property is owned by Mr. Dale's pension fund. It is available on short or long lease or is for sale depending on the requirements of the purchaser.

5.6   Included in motor vehicles is a 1973 Jensen Interceptor MKIII with a WDV of £1. This would be removed from the company at book value and excluded from the sale of the company.

APPENDICES (to be added as attachments)

I   Organisation Chart
II   Major Items of Plant & Equipment
III   Market Sector Activities
IV   Audited Accounts for the Year Ended 30th April 2010
V   Financial Projections for the Three Years Ended 30th April 2013 (see page 99)
VI   Product Technical Specifications
VII   Promotional Literature

Appendix III

Good Business Limited

Financial Projections
To 30th April 2013

99

Good Business Limited

Annual Profit Summaries for the
Five Years Ending 30th April 2013

	Actual 2009 £	Sales %	Actual 2010 £	Annual Increase %	2011 £	Annual Increase %	2012 £	Annual Increase %	2013 £	Annual Increase %
Sales										
Factored	1,772,718	48.2%	1,805,987	1.9%	1,842,722	2.0%	1,873,933	1.7%	1,905,790	1.7%
Manufactured	1,905,089	51.8%	2,158,688	13.3%	2,357,988	9.2%	2,578,929	9.4%	2,811,032	9.0%
	3,677,807		3,964,675	7.8%	4,200,710	6.0%	4,452,862	6.0%	4,716,822	5.9%
Cost of Sales										
Purchases	960,625	26.1%	989,943	3.1%	1,031,694	4.2%	1,079,819	4.7%	1,132,037	4.8%
Consumables	146,261	4.0%	157,176	7.5%	166,768	6.1%	176,779	6.0%	187,258	5.9%
Repairs & Renewals	37,999	1.0%	40,202	5.8%	37,367	-7.1%	39,235	5.0%	41,001	4.5%
Power	87,012	2.4%	93,729	7.7%	97,954	4.5%	102,852	5.0%	108,508	5.5%
Plant Hire	16,795	0.5%	18,645	11.0%	17,854	-4.2%	18,747	5.0%	19,778	5.5%
Transport	95,897	2.6%	98,844	3.1%	98,946	0.1%	103,893	5.0%	110,127	6.0%
Subcontractors	563,120	15.3%	600,901	6.7%	600,180	-0.1%	630,189	5.0%	671,151	6.5%
Direct labour	764,204	20.8%	816,459	6.8%	848,295	3.9%	878,209	3.5%	903,055	2.8%
Depreciation	15,399	0.4%	14,045	-8.8%	14,000	-0.3%	23,600	68.6%	39,600	67.8%
	2,687,312	73.1%	2,829,944	5.3%	2,913,058	2.9%	3,053,322	4.8%	3,212,516	5.2%
Gross Profit	990,495		1,134,731	14.6%	1,287,651	13.5%	1,399,540	8.7%	1,504,306	7.5%
Margin	26.9%		28.6%		30.7%		31.4%		31.9%	
Establishment Costs										
Light & Heat	31,543	0.9%	32,481	3.0%	33,475	3.1%	35,149	5.0%	36,906	5.0%
Rent & Rates	87,159	2.4%	91,702	5.2%	99,417	8.4%	104,388	5.0%	123,178	18.0%
Insurance	24,021	0.7%	24,957	3.9%	25,139	0.7%	26,396	5.0%	27,980	6.0%
Repairs	3,575	0.1%	2,759	-22.8%	3,650	32.3%	3,833	5.0%	4,043	5.6%
	146,298	4.0%	151,899	3.8%	161,681	6.4%	169,765	5.0%	192,107	13.2%
Selling Costs										
Advertising & Sponsorship	62,693	1.7%	68,217	8.8%	75,009	10.0%	81,000	8.0%	85,860	6.0%
Travelling & Entertainment	4,657	0.1%	4,865	4.5%	5,611	15.3%	7,200	28.3%	7,704	7.0%
Motor Expenses	11,932	0.3%	12,909	8.2%	15,855	22.8%	21,000	32.5%	22,260	6.0%
Salesmen's Wages	56,064	1.5%	57,849	3.2%	59,046	2.1%	88,320	49.6%	94,502	7.0%
Commissions	23,431	0.6%	25,717	9.8%	27,643	7.5%	30,000	8.5%	32,100	7.0%
Depreciation	14,944	0.4%	14,944	0.0%	15,000	0.4%	19,200	28.0%	28,200	46.9%
	173,721	4.7%	184,501	6.2%	198,164	7.4%	246,720	24.5%	270,626	9.7%
Administration Expenses										
Directors' Remuneration	93,670	2.5%	93,670	0.0%	104,497	11.6%	104,496	0.0%	110,766	6.0%
Directors' Expenses	23,232	0.6%	26,155	12.6%	27,762	6.1%	30,000	8.1%	30,000	0.0%
Directors' Pensions	20,000	0.5%	20,000	0.0%	24,000	20.0%	24,000	0.0%	24,000	0.0%
	136,902	3.7%	139,825	2.1%	156,259	11.8%	158,496	1.4%	164,766	4.0%
Printing & Stationery	3,659	0.1%	4,011	9.6%	4,236	5.6%	4,380	3.4%	4,643	6.0%
Postage	938	0.0%	998	6.4%	1,201	20.3%	1,260	4.9%	1,336	6.0%
Sundry Expenses	8,508	0.2%	9,104	7.0%	9,659	6.1%	9,840	1.9%	10,430	6.0%
Telephone	2,873	0.1%	3,176	10.5%	4,244	33.6%	4,380	3.2%	4,643	6.0%
Office Wages	108,236	2.9%	118,875	9.8%	130,849	10.1%	136,200	4.1%	145,734	7.0%
Staff Welfare	3,989	0.1%	4,059	1.8%	4,205	3.6%	4,380	4.2%	4,643	6.0%
Audit & Accountancy	4,980	0.1%	5,100	2.4%	5,400	5.9%	5,640	4.4%	6,000	6.4%
Legal & Professional	4,282	0.1%	6,878	60.6%	5,120	-25.6%	5,400	5.5%	5,700	5.6%
Bank Charges	2,841	0.1%	3,151	10.9%	3,302	4.8%	3,480	5.4%	3,720	6.9%
Depreciation	1,612	0.0%	1,612	0.0%	1,800	11.7%	1,920	6.7%	2,035	6.0%
	278,820	7.6%	296,789	6.4%	326,275	9.9%	335,376	2.8%	353,649	5.4%
Operating Profit	391,656	10.6%	501,542	28.1%	601,531	19.9%	647,679	7.7%	687,924	6.2%
Interest (Paid)/Received	(22,783)	-0.6%	(8,840)	-61.2%	2,654	-130.0%	15,771	494.2%	26,232	61.6%
Profit Before Tax	£368,873	10.0%	£492,702	33.6%	£604,185	22.6%	£663,450	9.6%	£714,156	7.5%
Corporation Tax	95,907	2.6%	152,738	59.3%	187,298	22.6%	205,669	9.8%	221,388	7.5%
Dividends	100,000	2.7%	120,000	20.0%	150,000	25.0%	200,000	33.3%	250,000	25.0%
Retained Profit	£172,966	4.7%	£219,964	27.2%	£266,887	21.3%	£257,781	-3.4%	£242,768	-6.0%

Good Business Limited

Profit Forecast for the Year Ending 30th April 2011

	Actual 3 months to Jul £	Aug £	Sep £	Oct £	Nov £	Dec £	Jan £	Feb £	Mar £	Apr £	Total
Sales											
Factored	553,247	184,211	221,053	202,632	165,790	55,263	73,684	110,526	128,947	147,369	1,842,722
Manufactured	710,909	235,297	282,356	258,827	211,767	70,589	94,119	141,178	164,708	188,238	2,357,988
	1,264,156	419,508	503,409	461,458	377,557	125,852	167,803	251,705	293,655	335,606	4,200,710
Cost of Sales											
Purchases	310,477	103,031	123,637	113,334	92,728	30,909	41,212	61,819	72,122	82,425	1,031,694
Consumables	50,187	16,654	19,985	18,320	14,989	4,996	6,662	9,993	11,658	13,324	166,768
Repairs & Renewals	10,367	3,000	3,000	3,000	3,000	3,000	3,000	3,000	3,000	3,000	37,367
Power	24,540	10,488	12,585	11,536	9,439	3,146	4,195	6,293	7,341	8,390	97,954
Plant Hire	4,354	1,500	1,500	1,500	1,500	1,500	1,500	1,500	1,500	1,500	17,854
Transport	25,532	10,488	12,585	11,536	9,439	3,146	4,195	6,293	7,341	8,390	98,946
Subcontractors	159,697	62,926	75,511	69,219	56,634	18,878	25,170	37,756	44,048	50,341	600,180
Direct labour	212,301	70,666	70,666	70,666	70,666	70,666	70,666	70,666	70,666	70,666	848,295
Depreciation	3,200	1,200	1,200	1,200	1,200	1,200	1,200	1,200	1,200	1,200	14,000
	800,655	279,953	320,670	300,312	259,594	137,442	157,801	198,518	218,877	239,236	2,913,058
Gross Profit	463,501	139,555	182,739	161,147	117,963	(11,590)	10,002	53,186	74,778	96,370	1,287,651
Margin	36.7%	33.3%	36.3%	34.9%	31.2%	-9.2%	6.0%	21.1%	25.5%	28.7%	30.7%
Establishment Costs											
Light & Heat	8,455	2,780	2,780	2,780	2,780	2,780	2,780	2,780	2,780	2,780	33,475
Rent & Rates	30,567	7,650	7,650	7,650	7,650	7,650	7,650	7,650	7,650	7,650	99,417
Insurance	6,239	2,100	2,100	2,100	2,100	2,100	2,100	2,100	2,100	2,100	25,139
Repairs	950	300	300	300	300	300	300	300	300	300	3,650
	46,211	12,830	12,830	12,830	12,830	12,830	12,830	12,830	12,830	12,830	161,681
Selling Costs											
Advertising & Sponsorship	18,759	6,250	6,250	6,250	6,250	6,250	6,250	6,250	6,250	6,250	75,009
Travelling & Entertainment	211	600	600	600	600	600	600	600	600	600	5,611
Motor Expenses	4,605	1,250	1,250	1,250	1,250	1,250	1,250	1,250	1,250	1,250	15,855
Salesmen's Wages	14,946	4,900	4,900	4,900	4,900	4,900	4,900	4,900	4,900	4,900	59,046
Commissions	6,943	2,300	2,300	2,300	2,300	2,300	2,300	2,300	2,300	2,300	27,643
Depreciation	3,750	1,250	1,250	1,250	1,250	1,250	1,250	1,250	1,250	1,250	15,000
	49,214	16,550	16,550	16,550	16,550	16,550	16,550	16,550	16,550	16,550	198,164
Administration Expenses											
Directors' Remuneration	26,125	8,708	8,708	8,708	8,708	8,708	8,708	8,708	8,708	8,708	104,497
Directors' Expenses	7,062	2,300	2,300	2,300	2,300	2,300	2,300	2,300	2,300	2,300	27,762
Directors' Pensions	6,000	2,000	2,000	2,000	2,000	2,000	2,000	2,000	2,000	2,000	24,000
	39,187	13,008	13,008	13,008	13,008	13,008	13,008	13,008	13,008	13,008	156,259
Printing & Stationery	1,086	350	350	350	350	350	350	350	350	350	4,236
Postage	301	100	100	100	100	100	100	100	100	100	1,201
Sundry Expenses	2,639	780	780	780	780	780	780	780	780	780	9,659
Telephone	1,094	350	350	350	350	350	350	350	350	350	4,244
Office Wages	32,749	10,900	10,900	10,900	10,900	10,900	10,900	10,900	10,900	10,900	130,849
Staff Welfare	1,055	350	350	350	350	350	350	350	350	350	4,205
Audit & Accountancy	1,350	450	450	450	450	450	450	450	450	450	5,400
Legal & Professional	1,295	425	425	425	425	425	425	425	425	425	5,120
Bank Charges	827	275	275	275	275	275	275	275	275	275	3,302
Depreciation	450	150	150	150	150	150	150	150	150	150	1,800
	82,033	27,138	27,138	27,138	27,138	27,138	27,138	27,138	27,138	27,138	326,275
Operating Profit	286,043	83,037	126,221	104,629	61,445	(68,108)	(46,516)	(3,332)	18,260	39,852	601,531
Interest Received	(751)	(102)	328	1,030	1,356	1,582	257	(543)	(438)	(65)	2,654
Profit Before Tax	£285,292	£82,935	£126,549	£105,658	£62,801	(£66,525)	(£46,259)	(£3,875)	£17,822	£39,787	£604,185

Good Business Limited

page

Profit Forecast for the Year Ending 30th April 2012

	May £	Jun £	Jul £	Aug £	Sep £	Oct £	Nov £	Dec £	Jan £	Feb £	Mar £	Apr £	Total £
Sales													
Factored	184,530	187,916	186,223	187,895	225,474	206,684	169,105	56,368	75,158	112,737	131,526	150,316	1,873,93
Manufactured	253,389	258,039	255,714	258,827	310,592	284,709	232,944	77,648	103,531	155,296	181,179	207,061	2,578,92
	437,919	445,955	441,937	446,722	536,066	491,394	402,049	134,016	178,689	268,033	312,705	357,377	4,452,86
Cost of Sales													
Purchases	106,195	108,144	107,170	108,330	129,996	119,163	97,497	32,499	43,332	64,998	75,831	86,664	1,079,81
Consumables	17,385	17,704	17,545	17,735	21,282	19,508	15,961	5,320	7,094	10,641	12,414	14,188	176,77
Repairs & Renewals	3,270	3,270	3,270	3,270	3,270	3,270	3,270	3,270	3,270	3,270	3,270	3,270	39,23
Power	8,571	8,571	8,571	8,571	8,571	8,571	8,571	8,571	8,571	8,571	8,571	8,571	102,85
Plant Hire	1,562	1,562	1,562	1,562	1,562	1,562	1,562	1,562	1,562	1,562	1,562	1,562	18,74
Transport	8,658	8,658	8,658	8,658	8,658	8,658	8,658	8,658	8,658	8,658	8,658	8,658	103,89
Subcontractors	52,516	52,516	52,516	52,516	52,516	52,516	52,516	52,516	52,516	52,516	52,516	52,516	630,18
Direct labour	74,226	74,226	74,226	74,226	74,226	74,226	74,226	74,226	74,226	70,059	70,059	70,059	878,20
Depreciation	1,300	1,300	1,300	1,300	1,300	1,300	1,300	1,300	1,300	3,300	3,300	3,300	23,60
	273,683	275,950	274,817	276,167	301,380	288,773	263,560	187,922	202,528	223,574	236,181	248,787	3,053,3.
Gross Profit	164,236	170,004	167,120	170,555	234,686	202,620	138,489	(53,905)	(23,839)	44,459	76,525	108,590	1,399,5
Margin	37.5%	38.1%	37.8%	38.2%	43.8%	41.2%	0	-40.2%	-13.3%	16.6%	24.5%	30.4%	31.
Establishment Costs													
Light & Heat	2,929	2,929	2,929	2,929	2,929	2,929	2,929	2,929	2,929	2,929	2,929	2,929	35,1
Rent & Rates	8,699	8,699	8,699	8,699	8,699	8,699	8,699	8,699	8,699	8,699	8,699	8,699	104,3
Insurance	2,200	2,200	2,200	2,200	2,200	2,200	2,200	2,200	2,200	2,200	2,200	2,200	26,3
Repairs	319	319	319	319	319	319	319	319	319	319	319	319	3,8
	14,147	14,147	14,147	14,147	14,147	14,147	14,147	14,147	14,147	14,147	14,147	14,147	169,
Selling Costs													
Advertising & Sponsc	6,750	6,750	6,750	6,750	6,750	6,750	6,750	6,750	6,750	6,750	6,750	6,750	81,
Travelling & Entertain	600	600	600	600	600	600	600	600	600	600	600	600	7,
Motor Expenses	1,750	1,750	1,750	1,750	1,750	1,750	1,750	1,750	1,750	1,750	1,750	1,750	21,0
Salesmen's Wages	7,360	7,360	7,360	7,360	7,360	7,360	7,360	7,360	7,360	7,360	7,360	7,360	88,
Commissions	2,500	2,500	2,500	2,500	2,500	2,500	2,500	2,500	2,500	2,500	2,500	2,500	30,
Depreciation	1,600	1,600	1,600	1,600	1,600	1,600	1,600	1,600	1,600	1,600	1,600	1,600	19,
	20,560	20,560	20,560	20,560	20,560	20,560	20,560	20,560	20,560	20,560	20,560	20,560	246,
Administration Expenses													
Directors' Remunerat	8,708	8,708	8,708	8,708	8,708	8,708	8,708	8,708	8,708	8,708	8,708	8,708	104,
Directors' Expenses	2,500	2,500	2,500	2,500	2,500	2,500	2,500	2,500	2,500	2,500	2,500	2,500	30,
Directors' Pensions	2,000	2,000	2,000	2,000	2,000	2,000	2,000	2,000	2,000	2,000	2,000	2,000	24,
	13,208	13,208	13,208	13,208	13,208	13,208	13,208	13,208	13,208	13,208	13,208	13,208	158
Printing & Stationery	365	365	365	365	365	365	365	365	365	365	365	365	4
Postage	105	105	105	105	105	105	105	105	105	105	105	105	1
Sundry Expenses	820	820	820	820	820	820	820	820	820	820	820	820	9
Telephone	365	365	365	365	365	365	365	365	365	365	365	365	4
Office Wages	11,350	11,350	11,350	11,350	11,350	11,350	11,350	11,350	11,350	11,350	11,350	11,350	136
Staff Welfare	365	365	365	365	365	365	365	365	365	365	365	365	4
Audit & Accountancy	470	470	470	470	470	470	470	470	470	470	470	470	5
Legal & Professional	450	450	450	450	450	450	450	450	450	450	450	450	5
Bank Charges	290	290	290	290	290	290	290	290	290	290	290	290	3
Depreciation	160	160	160	160	160	160	160	160	160	160	160	160	1
	27,948	27,948	27,948	27,948	27,948	27,948	27,948	27,948	27,948	27,948	27,948	27,948	335
Operating Profit	101,581	107,349	104,465	107,900	172,031	139,965	75,834	(116,560)	(86,495)	(18,196)	13,870	45,935	647
Interest Received	(71)	410	1,139	1,296	1,795	2,580	2,964	3,370	1,094	351	289	557	15
Profit Before Tax	£101,510	£107,759	£105,604	£109,196	£173,826	£142,545	£78,798	(£113,190)	(£85,401)	(£17,845)	£14,159	£46,492	£663

Good Business Limited

page 4

Profit Forecast for the Year Ending 30th April 2013

	May £	Jun £	Jul £	Aug £	Sep £	Oct £	Nov £	Dec £	Jan £	Feb £	Mar £	Apr £	Total £
Sales													
Factored	187,667	191,110	189,389	191,089	229,307	210,198	171,980	57,327	76,436	114,653	133,762	152,871	1,905,790
Manufactured	276,194	281,262	278,728	282,121	338,545	310,333	253,909	84,636	112,848	169,273	197,485	225,697	2,811,032
	463,861	472,373	468,117	473,210	567,852	520,531	425,889	141,963	189,284	283,926	331,247	378,568	4,716,822
Cost of Sales													
Purchases	111,327	113,369	112,348	113,570	136,285	124,927	102,213	34,071	45,428	68,142	79,499	90,856	1,132,037
Consumables	18,415	18,753	18,584	18,786	22,544	20,665	16,908	5,636	7,515	11,272	13,151	15,029	187,258
Repairs & Renewals	3,417	3,417	3,417	3,417	3,417	3,417	3,417	3,417	3,417	3,417	3,417	3,417	41,001
Power	9,042	9,042	9,042	9,042	9,042	9,042	9,042	9,042	9,042	9,042	9,042	9,042	108,508
Plant Hire	1,648	1,648	1,648	1,648	1,648	1,648	1,648	1,648	1,648	1,648	1,648	1,648	19,778
Transport	9,177	9,177	9,177	9,177	9,177	9,177	9,177	9,177	9,177	9,177	9,177	9,177	110,127
Subcontractors	55,929	55,929	55,929	55,929	55,929	55,929	55,929	55,929	55,929	55,929	55,929	55,929	671,151
Direct labour	75,255	75,255	75,255	75,255	75,255	75,255	75,255	75,255	75,255	75,255	75,255	75,255	903,055
Depreciation	3,300	3,300	3,300	3,300	3,300	3,300	3,300	3,300	3,300	3,300	3,300	3,300	39,600
	287,510	289,091	288,701	290,125	316,597	303,361	276,890	197,475	210,711	237,183	250,418	263,654	3,212,516
Gross Profit	176,351	182,482	179,416	183,085	251,256	217,170	149,000	(55,512)	(21,427)	46,744	80,829	114,914	1,504,306
Margin	38.0%	38.6%	38.3%	38.7%	44.2%	41.7%	0	-39.1%	-11.3%	16.5%	24.4%	30.4%	31.9%
Establishment Costs													
Light & Heat	3,076	3,076	3,076	3,076	3,076	3,076	3,076	3,076	3,076	3,076	3,076	3,076	36,906
Rent & Rates	10,265	10,265	10,265	10,265	10,265	10,265	10,265	10,265	10,265	10,265	10,265	10,265	123,178
Insurance	2,332	2,332	2,332	2,332	2,332	2,332	2,332	2,332	2,332	2,332	2,332	2,332	27,980
Repairs	337	337	337	337	337	337	337	337	337	337	337	337	4,043
	16,009	16,009	16,009	16,009	16,009	16,009	16,009	16,009	16,009	16,009	16,009	16,009	192,107
Selling Costs													
Advertising & Sponsc	7,155	7,155	7,155	7,155	7,155	7,155	7,155	7,155	7,155	7,155	7,155	7,155	85,860
Travelling & Entertain	642	642	642	642	642	642	642	642	642	642	642	642	7,704
Motor Expenses	1,855	1,855	1,855	1,855	1,855	1,855	1,855	1,855	1,855	1,855	1,855	1,855	22,260
Salesmen's Wages	7,875	7,875	7,875	7,875	7,875	7,875	7,875	7,875	7,875	7,875	7,875	7,875	94,502
Commissions	2,675	2,675	2,675	2,675	2,675	2,675	2,675	2,675	2,675	2,675	2,675	2,675	32,100
Depreciation	2,350	2,350	2,350	2,350	2,350	2,350	2,350	2,350	2,350	2,350	2,350	2,350	28,200
	22,552	22,552	22,552	22,552	22,552	22,552	22,552	22,552	22,552	22,552	22,552	22,552	270,626
Administration Expenses													
Directors' Remunerat	9,230	9,230	9,230	9,230	9,230	9,230	9,230	9,230	9,230	9,230	9,230	9,230	110,766
Directors' Expenses	2,500	2,500	2,500	2,500	2,500	2,500	2,500	2,500	2,500	2,500	2,500	2,500	30,000
Directors' Pensions	2,000	2,000	2,000	2,000	2,000	2,000	2,000	2,000	2,000	2,000	2,000	2,000	24,000
	13,730	13,730	13,730	13,730	13,730	13,730	13,730	13,730	13,730	13,730	13,730	13,730	164,766
Printing & Stationery	387	387	387	387	387	387	387	387	387	387	387	387	4,643
Postage	111	111	111	111	111	111	111	111	111	111	111	111	1,336
Sundry Expenses	869	869	869	869	869	869	869	869	869	869	869	869	10,430
Telephone	387	387	387	387	387	387	387	387	387	387	387	387	4,643
Office Wages	12,145	12,145	12,145	12,145	12,145	12,145	12,145	12,145	12,145	12,145	12,145	12,145	145,734
Staff Welfare	387	387	387	387	387	387	387	387	387	387	387	387	4,643
Audit & Accountancy	500	500	500	500	500	500	500	500	500	500	500	500	6,000
Legal & Professional	475	475	475	475	475	475	475	475	475	475	475	475	5,700
Bank Charges	310	310	310	310	310	310	310	310	310	310	310	310	3,720
Depreciation	170	170	170	170	170	170	170	170	170	170	170	170	2,035
	29,471	29,471	29,471	29,471	29,471	29,471	29,471	29,471	29,471	29,471	29,471	29,471	353,649
Operating Profit	108,319	114,450	111,384	115,053	183,224	149,138	80,968	(123,544)	(89,459)	(21,288)	12,797	46,882	687,924
Interest Received	447	930	1,723	1,906	2,442	3,292	3,715	4,154	2,276	1,492	1,416	1,701	26,202
Profit Before Tax	£108,766	£115,380	£113,107	£116,959	£185,666	£152,430	£84,683	(£119,390)	(£87,183)	(£19,796)	£14,213	£48,583	£714,156

Good Business Limited

Annual Balance Sheet forecasts
As At 30 April

	Actual 2009 £	Actual 2010 £	2011 £	2012 £	2013 £
Fixed Assets					
Plant & Equipment	238,936	267,796	267,796	492,796	492,796
Fixtures, Fittings etc	10,624	11,294	11,294	11,294	11,294
Motor Vehicles	59,770	59,770	59,770	59,770	77,770
	309,330	338,860	338,860	563,860	581,860
Accumulated Depreciation	95,265	125,866	156,666	201,386	271,221
	214,065	212,994	182,194	362,474	310,639
Current Assets					
Stocks & WIP	384,939	465,380	470,493	475,718	362,349
Trade Debtors	806,232	873,228	981,212	1,017,985	1,053,778
Prepayments	37,312	39,116	39,116	39,116	39,116
Bank Account	0	0	(17,820)	152,253	516,031
	1,228,483	1,377,724	1,473,002	1,685,072	1,971,274
Current Liabilities					
Trade Creditors	457,966	435,444	283,459	348,295	269,182
Accruals	18,135	18,342	18,642	18,882	19,242
Corporation Tax	95,907	152,738	187,298	205,669	221,388
Proposed Dividend	100,000	120,000	150,000	200,000	250,000
Bank Overdraft	247,789	113,840	0	0	0
VAT	67,832	73,129	71,683	72,806	77,439
PAYE & NIC	34,370	36,706	36,706	36,706	36,706
	1,021,993	950,199	747,788	882,358	873,957
Net Current Assets	206,490	427,525	725,213	802,714	1,097,317
Assets Employed	420,555	640,519	907,408	1,165,188	1,407,955
Shareholders Funds					
Share Capital	20,000	20,000	20,000	20,000	20,000
Reserves	227,589	400,555	620,520	887,408	1,095,188
Profit & Loss A/c	172,966	219,964	266,888	257,780	242,258
	420,555	640,519	907,408	1,165,188	1,357,446

Good Business Limited

Monthly Balance Sheet Forecasts for the Year Ending 30th April 2011

	Jul £	Aug £	Sep £	Oct £	Nov £	Dec £	Jan £	Feb £	Mar £	Apr £
Fixed Assets										
Plant & Equipment	267,796	267,796	267,796	267,796	267,796	267,796	267,796	267,796	267,796	267,796
Fixtures, Fittings etc	11,294	11,294	11,294	11,294	11,294	11,294	11,294	11,294	11,294	11,294
Motor Vehicles	59,770	59,770	59,770	59,770	59,770	59,770	59,770	59,770	59,770	59,770
	338,860	338,860	338,860	338,860	338,860	338,860	338,860	338,860	338,860	338,860
Accumulated Depreciation	133,266	135,866	138,466	141,066	143,666	146,266	148,866	151,466	154,066	156,666
	205,594	202,994	200,394	197,794	195,194	192,594	189,994	187,394	184,794	182,194
Current Assets										
Stocks & WIP	485,986	475,683	455,077	393,258	403,561	424,168	434,471	444,774	468,544	470,493
Trade Debtors	1,143,974	1,153,291	1,252,319	1,252,319	1,129,089	784,044	685,460	808,690	907,274	981,212
Prepayments	58,016	48,266	61,466	51,716	41,966	55,166	45,416	35,666	48,866	39,116
Bank Account	(68,996)	(27,800)	89,828	281,561	370,895	432,752	70,248	(148,496)	(119,828)	(17,820)
	1,618,980	1,649,441	1,858,690	1,978,854	1,945,512	1,696,129	1,235,594	1,140,634	1,304,857	1,473,001
Current Liabilities										
Trade Creditors	456,050	478,873	515,735	493,282	479,664	284,977	127,830	66,368	185,825	283,459
Accruals	19,692	20,142	20,592	15,942	16,392	16,842	17,292	17,742	18,192	18,642
Corporation Tax	152,738	152,738	152,738	152,738	152,738	152,738	0	0	0	0
Proposed Dividend	120,000	120,000	120,000	120,000	120,000	120,000	0	0	0	0
Bank Overdraft	0	0	0	0	0	0	0	0	0	0
VAT	113,577	35,230	78,018	117,027	31,452	40,232	52,790	20,116	44,010	71,683
PAYE & NIC	36,706	36,706	36,706	36,706	36,706	36,706	36,706	36,706	36,706	36,706
	898,763	843,689	923,789	935,695	836,952	651,495	234,618	140,932	284,733	410,490
Net Current Assets	720,217	805,752	934,901	1,043,160	1,108,560	1,044,635	1,000,976	999,702	1,020,123	1,062,511
Assets Employed	925,811	1,008,746	1,135,295	1,240,954	1,303,754	1,237,229	1,190,970	1,187,096	1,204,917	1,244,705
Shareholders Funds										
Share Capital	20,000	20,000	20,000	20,000	20,000	20,000	20,000	20,000	20,000	20,000
Reserves	620,520	620,520	620,520	620,520	620,520	620,520	620,520	620,520	620,520	620,520
Profit & Loss A/c	285,292	368,227	494,776	600,434	663,235	596,710	550,451	546,576	564,398	604,186
	925,812	1,008,747	1,135,296	1,240,954	1,303,755	1,237,230	1,190,971	1,187,096	1,204,918	1,244,706

Corporation Tax	187,298
Dividend	150,000
	907,408

Good Business Limited

Monthly Balance Sheet Forecasts for the Year Ending 30th April 2012

	May £	Jun £	Jul £	Aug £	Sep £	Oct £	Nov £	Dec £	Jan £	Feb £	Mar £	Apr £
Fixed Assets												
Plant & Equipment	267,796	267,796	267,796	267,796	267,796	267,796	267,796	267,796	492,796	492,796	492,796	492,798
Fixtures, Fittings etc	11,294	11,294	11,294	11,294	11,294	11,294	11,294	11,294	11,294	11,294	11,294	11,294
Motor Vehicles	59,770	59,770	59,770	59,770	59,770	59,770	59,770	59,770	59,770	59,770	59,770	59,770
	338,860	338,860	338,860	338,860	338,860	338,860	338,860	338,860	563,860	563,860	563,860	563,860
Accumulated Depreciation	159,726	162,786	165,846	168,906	171,966	175,026	178,086	181,146	186,206	191,266	196,326	201,386
	179,134	176,074	173,014	169,954	166,894	163,834	160,774	157,714	377,654	372,594	367,534	362,474
Current Assets												
Stocks & WIP	469,519	470,679	492,345	481,512	459,846	394,848	405,681	427,347	438,180	449,013	473,676	475,711
Trade Debtors	1,126,076	1,195,627	1,195,627	1,198,888	1,306,679	1,306,679	1,175,455	808,026	703,047	834,271	939,251	1,017,98
Prepayments	54,613	69,812	58,913	48,014	63,213	52,314	41,415	56,614	45,715	34,816	50,015	39,11
Bank Account	(19,516)	112,084	311,419	354,296	490,869	705,557	810,543	921,622	299,077	95,907	78,936	152,25
	1,630,692	1,848,201	2,058,304	2,082,711	2,320,607	2,459,398	2,433,094	2,213,609	1,486,018	1,414,007	1,541,877	1,685,07
Current Liabilities												
Trade Creditors	367,796	433,010	493,476	485,561	493,775	445,176	441,197	329,549	236,694	203,089	287,002	348,29
Accruals	19,112	19,582	20,052	20,522	20,992	16,062	16,532	17,002	17,472	17,942	18,412	18,88
Corporation Tax	187,298	187,298	187,298	187,298	187,298	187,298	187,298	187,298	0	0	0	
Proposed Dividend	150,000	150,000	150,000	150,000	150,000	150,000	150,000	150,000	0	0	0	
Bank Overdraft	0	0	0	0	0	0	0	0	0	0	0	
VAT	39,998	81,004	121,507	41,103	93,429	140,144	35,492	37,314	44,749	18,657	42,926	72,80
PAYE & NIC	36,706	36,706	36,706	36,706	36,706	36,706	36,706	36,706	36,706	36,706	36,706	36,7
	800,910	907,600	1,009,039	921,190	982,200	975,386	867,225	757,869	335,621	276,394	305,046	476,6
Net Current Assets	829,783	940,602	1,049,266	1,161,521	1,338,407	1,484,012	1,565,870	1,455,739	1,150,398	1,137,613	1,156,831	1,208,3
Assets Employed	1,008,917	1,116,676	1,222,280	1,331,475	1,505,301	1,647,846	1,726,644	1,613,453	1,528,052	1,510,207	1,524,365	1,570,8
Shareholders Funds												
Share Capital	20,000	20,000	20,000	20,000	20,000	20,000	20,000	20,000	20,000	20,000	20,000	20,0
Reserves	887,408	887,408	887,408	887,408	887,408	887,408	887,408	887,408	887,408	887,408	887,408	887,4
Profit & Loss A/c	101,510	209,269	314,873	424,068	597,893	740,438	819,236	706,046	620,645	602,800	616,958	663,4
	1,008,918	1,116,677	1,222,281	1,331,476	1,505,301	1,647,846	1,726,644	1,613,454	1,528,053	1,510,208	1,524,366	1,570,8

Corporation Tax 205,8
Dividend 200,0
1,165,

Good Business Limited

Monthly Balance Sheet Forecasts for the Year Ending 30th April 2013

	May £	Jun £	Jul £	Aug £	Sep £	Oct £	Nov £	Dec £	Jan £	Feb £	Mar £	Apr £
ixed Assets												
Plant & Equipment	492,796	492,796	492,796	492,796	492,796	492,796	492,796	492,796	492,796	492,796	492,796	492,796
Fixtures, Fittings etc	11,294	11,294	11,294	11,294	11,294	11,294	11,294	11,294	11,294	11,294	11,294	11,294
Motor Vehicles	77,770	77,770	77,770	77,770	77,770	77,770	77,770	77,770	77,770	77,770	77,770	77,770
	581,860	581,860	581,860	581,860	581,860	581,860	581,860	581,860	581,860	581,860	581,860	581,860
Accumulated Depreciation	207,206	213,025	218,845	224,664	230,484	236,304	242,123	247,943	253,762	259,582	265,402	271,221
	374,654	368,835	363,015	357,196	351,376	345,556	339,737	333,917	328,098	322,278	316,458	310,639
urrent Assets												
Stocks & WIP	474,697	475,919	498,633	487,276	464,562	396,420	407,777	430,491	441,848	453,205	362,349	362,349
Trade Debtors	1,169,349	1,241,909	1,241,909	1,245,393	1,359,590	1,359,590	1,220,585	831,369	720,165	859,170	970,375	1,053,778
Prepayments	54,499	72,697	60,101	47,504	65,702	53,106	40,509	58,707	46,111	33,514	51,712	39,116
Bank Account	122,129	254,472	471,149	521,123	667,730	900,335	1,016,112	1,136,045	622,367	408,060	387,211	465,293
	1,820,674	2,044,997	2,271,792	2,301,296	2,557,584	2,709,451	2,684,983	2,456,612	1,830,491	1,753,949	1,771,647	1,920,536
urrent Liabilities												
Trade Creditors	417,089	476,110	540,413	532,128	540,793	489,877	485,682	368,428	270,922	235,623	206,975	269,182
Accruals	19,302	19,882	20,382	20,882	21,382	16,242	16,742	17,242	17,742	18,242	18,742	19,242
Corporation Tax	205,669	205,669	205,669	205,669	205,669	205,669	205,669	205,669	0	0	0	0
Proposed Dividend	200,000	200,000	200,000	200,000	200,000	200,000	200,000	200,000	0	0	0	0
Bank Overdraft	0	0	0	0	0	0	0	0	0	0	0	0
VAT	42,529	86,131	129,197	43,708	99,345	149,018	37,743	39,696	47,614	19,848	45,661	77,439
PAYE & NIC	36,706	36,706	36,706	36,706	36,706	36,706	36,706	36,706	36,706	36,706	36,706	36,706
	921,375	1,024,498	1,132,367	1,039,093	1,103,895	1,097,512	982,542	867,741	372,984	310,419	308,084	402,569
t Current Assets	899,299	1,020,499	1,139,425	1,262,204	1,453,689	1,611,939	1,702,441	1,588,871	1,507,691	1,493,898	1,514,116	1,568,705
sets Employed	1,273,953	1,389,334	1,502,440	1,619,400	1,805,065	1,957,495	2,042,178	1,922,788	1,835,789	1,816,176	1,830,574	1,879,344
areholders Funds												
hare Capital	20,000	20,000	20,000	20,000	20,000	20,000	20,000	20,000	20,000	20,000	20,000	20,000
eserves	1,145,188	1,145,188	1,145,188	1,145,188	1,145,188	1,145,188	1,145,188	1,145,188	1,145,188	1,145,188	1,145,188	1,145,188
rofit & Loss A/c	108,766	224,146	337,253	454,212	639,877	792,307	876,991	757,600	670,601	650,989	665,386	714,156
	1,273,954	1,389,334	1,502,441	1,619,400	1,805,065	1,957,495	2,042,179	1,922,788	1,835,789	1,816,177	1,830,574	1,879,344

Corporation Tax	221,388
Dividend	250,000
	1,407,956

Good Business Limited

Cashflow Forecast for the Year Ending 30th April 2011

	Actual 3 months to Jul £	Aug £	Sep £	Oct £	Nov £	Dec £	Jan £	Feb £	Mar £	Apr £	Total
Receipts											
Debtors (45 days)	1,033,734	411,578	419,130	461,458	482,434	419,508	251,705	146,828	209,754	272,680	4,108,808
Vat @ 17.5%	180,903	72,026	73,348	80,755	84,426	73,414	44,048	25,695	36,707	47,719	719,041
	1,214,637	483,604	492,478	542,214	566,860	492,922	295,753	172,523	246,461	320,399	4,827,849
Payments											
Vatable Expenses (60 days)	615,144	190,000	210,000	205,048	218,192	258,909	238,551	197,833	75,681	96,040	2,305,398
Non Vat Expenses (Current)	11,287	3,705	3,705	3,705	3,705	3,705	3,705	3,705	3,705	3,705	44,632
Other Expenses											
Insurance	25,139										25,139
Rent & Rates	30,567		22,950			22,950			22,950		99,417
Audit & Accountancy				5,100							5,100
Wages +PAYE (Current)	306,126	101,774	101,774	101,774	101,774	101,774	101,774	101,774	101,774	101,774	1,222,092
Capital Expenditure:											
Plant & Equipment											0
Motor Vehicles											0
Corporation Tax							152,738				152,738
Dividends							120,000				120,000
Input Vat	107,650	33,250	36,750	35,883	38,184	45,309	41,746	34,621	13,244	16,807	403,444
Vat Quarterly Returns	73,129	113,577			117,027			52,790			356,523
	1,169,042	442,306	375,179	351,510	478,881	432,648	658,514	390,723	217,354	218,326	4,734,483
Bank Account											
Opening Balance	(113,840)	(68,996)	(27,800)	89,827	281,561	370,895	432,751	70,247	(148,497)	(119,829)	(113,840)
Movement in Month	45,595	41,298	117,299	190,703	87,979	60,274	(362,761)	(218,201)	29,106	102,073	93,366
	(68,245)	(27,698)	89,499	280,531	369,539	431,169	69,990	(147,954)	(119,391)	(17,755)	(20,474)
Interest @ 4.5%	(751)	(102)	328	1,030	1,356	1,582	257	(543)	(438)	(65)	2,654
Closing Balance	(68,996)	(27,800)	89,827	281,561	370,895	432,751	70,247	(148,497)	(119,829)	(17,820)	(17,820)

Good Business Limited

Cashflow Forecast for the Year Ending 30th April 2012

	May £	Jun £	Jul £	Aug £	Sep £	Oct £	Nov £	Dec £	Jan £	Feb £	Mar £	Apr £	Total £
Receipts													
Debtors (45 days)	314,631	386,763	441,937	443,946	444,329	491,394	513,730	446,722	268,033	156,353	223,361	290,369	4,421,568
Vat @ 17.5%	55,060	67,683	77,339	77,690	77,758	85,994	89,903	78,176	46,906	27,362	39,088	50,815	773,774
	369,691	454,446	519,276	521,636	522,087	577,388	603,633	524,898	314,939	183,715	262,449	341,184	5,195,342
Payments													
Vatable Expenses (60 days)	136,757	157,116	177,475	209,362	211,630	210,496	211,846	237,059	224,453	199,240	123,601	136,207	2,235,242
Non Vat Expenses (Current)	3,903	3,903	3,903	3,903	3,903	3,903	3,903	3,903	3,903	3,903	3,903	3,903	46,836
Other Expenses													
Insurance	26,396	0	0	0	0	0	0	0	0	0	0	0	26,396
Rent & Rates	0	26,097	0	0	26,097	0	0	26,097	0	0	26,097	0	104,388
Audit & Accountancy	0	0	0	0	0	5,400	0	0	0	0	0	0	5,400
Wages +PAYE (Current)	108,644	108,644	108,644	108,644	108,644	108,644	108,644	108,644	108,644	104,477	104,477	104,477	1,291,227
Capital Expenditure:													
Plant & Equipment	0	0	0	0	0	0	0	0	225,000	0	0	0	225,000
Motor Vehicles	0	0	0	0	0	0	0	0	0	0	0	0	0
Corporation Tax	0	0	0	0	0	0	0	0	187,298	0	0	0	187,298
Dividends	0	0	0	0	0	0	0	0	150,000	0	0	0	150,000
Input Vat	23,933	27,495	31,058	36,638	37,035	36,837	37,073	41,485	39,279	34,867	21,630	23,836	391,166
Vat Quarterly Returns	71,683	0	0	121,507	0	0	140,144	0	0	44,749	0	0	378,083
	371,316	323,255	321,080	480,054	387,309	365,280	501,610	417,188	938,577	387,236	279,708	268,423	5,041,036
Bank Account													
Opening Balance	(17,820)	(19,516)	112,084	311,419	354,296	490,869	705,557	810,543	921,622	299,077	95,907	78,936	(17,820)
Movement in Month	(1,625)	131,191	198,196	41,582	134,778	212,108	102,022	107,709	(623,638)	(203,521)	(17,259)	72,760	154,302
	(19,445)	111,675	310,280	353,001	489,074	702,977	807,579	918,252	297,984	95,556	78,648	151,696	136,482
Interest @ 4.5%	(71)	410	1,139	1,296	1,795	2,580	2,964	3,370	1,094	351	289	557	15,771
Closing Balance	(19,516)	112,084	311,419	354,296	490,869	705,557	810,543	921,622	299,077	95,907	78,936	152,253	152,253

Good Business Limited

Cashflow Forecast for the Year Ending 30th April 2013

	May £	Jun £	Jul £	Aug £	Sep £	Oct £	Nov £	Dec £	Jan £	Feb £	Mar £	Apr £	Total £
Receipts													
Debtors (45 days)	335,041	410,619	468,117	470,245	470,664	520,531	544,192	473,210	283,926	165,624	236,605	307,587	4,686,360
Vat @ 17 5%	58,632	71,858	81,920	82,293	82,366	91,093	95,234	82,812	49,687	28,984	41,406	53,828	820,113
	393,673	482,478	550,037	552,538	553,030	611,624	639,425	556,022	333,613	194,608	278,011	361,414	5,506,473
Payments													
Vatable Expenses (60 days)	161,420	174,027	186,633	220,837	223,218	222,027	223,452	249,923	236,688	210,216	130,802	144,038	2,383,281
Non Vat Expenses (Current)	4,109	4,109	4,109	4,109	4,109	4,109	4,109	4,109	4,109	4,109	4,109	4,109	49,312
Other Expenses													
Insurance	27,980												27,980
Rent & Rates		30,794			30,794			30,794			30,794		123,178
Audit & Accountancy						5,640							5,640
Wages +PAYE (Current)	111,680	111,680	111,680	111,680	111,680	111,680	111,680	111,680	111,680	111,680	111,680	111,680	1,340,158
Capital Expenditure													
Plant & Equipment													
Motor Vehicles	18,000												18,000
Corporation Tax								205,669					205,669
Dividends								200,000					200,000
Input Vat	28,249	30,455	32,661	38,646	39,063	38,855	39,104	43,737	41,420	36,788	22,890	25,207	417,074
Vat Quarterly Returns	72,806			129,197			149,018			47,614			398,635
	424,244	351,065	335,083	504,470	408,864	382,311	527,363	440,243	799,566	410,407	300,276	285,034	5,168,927
Bank Account													
Opening Balance	152,253	122,129	254,472	471,149	521,123	667,730	900,335	1,016,112	1,136,045	672,551	458,427	437,763	152,253
Movement in Month	(30,570)	131,413	214,954	48,068	144,165	229,313	112,062	115,778	(465,953)	(215,800)	(22,265)	76,381	337,546
	121,682	253,542	469,427	519,217	665,288	897,043	1,012,397	1,131,891	670,092	456,751	436,162	514,144	489,799
Interest @ 4 5%	447	930	1,723	1,906	2,442	3,292	3,715	4,154	2,459	1,676	1,601	1,887	26,231
Closing Balance	122,129	254,472	471,149	521,123	667,730	900,335	1,016,112	1,136,045	672,551	458,427	437,763	516,031	516,031

Good Business Limited

Assumptions

1 Inflation has been ignored.
2 Interest rates will remain constant.
3 VAT and Corporation Tax rates will remain constant.
4 There will be no change in the nature or seasonality of the trade.
5 The €:£ exchange rate will average 1.2
6 Customers will pay on average 45 days after invoicing.
7 Suppliers will be paid on average 60 days from date of supply.
8 VAT, PAYE, and NIC will be paid on time.
9 Wages and salaries will be paid in the month in which they are incurred.
10 Corporation Tax and dividends are ignored in the detailed P & L accounts.
11 New production staff and/or overtime will be available to meet requirements.
12 A new sales person will commence in May 2011.
13 A new automated finishing line will be installed in January 2012 producing salary savings of £50K pa.
14 Each year, approximately 7.5% of customers will convert to our manufactured product.
15 Suppliers of factored goods will hold prices to maintain market share.

Appendix IV

Sample Confidentiality Agreement

<u>STRICTLY PRIVATE & CONFIDENTIAL</u>

To: Potential Purchasers and Investors

<u>CONFIDENTIALITY UNDERTAKING AND INDEMNITY</u>

Gentlemen

The vendor, whose name will be disclosed, is going to provide you on a non-exclusive basis with information (verbal and written) to enable you, as a Potential Purchaser or Investor ("PPI"), to determine whether or not to pursue enquiries with a view to purchasing either shares in the company, the business or making loans or any other form of investment. The information may not be used for any other purpose.

The PPI accepts that the information does not and shall not be deemed to constitute any representation or warranty by anyone as to its accuracy, completeness or reasonableness. MacIntyre Hudson Corporate Finance Ltd ("MacIntyre Hudson") shall have no liability whatsoever to the PPI or anyone else resulting from the use of the information.

By signing this letter, the PPI acknowledges that the information provided is strictly confidential and that the vendor may suffer material commercial loss if such confidentiality is breached. The PPI agrees not to use any of such information for the PPI's own benefit (except in evaluating the investment potential of this particular sale) or for the benefit of others.

Except for information already in the public domain (other than as a result of a breach of this agreement), the PPI also agrees to keep permanently confidential the information provided and may not copy, reproduce or distribute to others any of the information without the prior written consent of the vendor. The PPI will, upon request, immediately return all information received in connection therewith, without retaining copies thereof following which the PPI will use its best efforts to prevent the disclosure of any information. The PPI also agrees not to make any announcements or disclose their prospective interest in the vendor or its business without the written consent of the vendor except where required by law or under the rules of a recognised Stock Exchange in which case the PPI agrees to consult with the vendor prior to such announcement.

The PPI agrees not to contact directly or indirectly the vendor, its employees or customers except with the explicit consent of MacIntyre Hudson.

The PPI hereby agree to indemnify and hold the vendor harmless from any loss which the vendor may incur or be subject to by reason of the breach of any provision of this letter by the PPI.

The PPI acknowledges that the vendors are acting in reliance upon the undertakings and indemnity set out above in the provision of information to the PPI.

You shall ensure that your employees, officers, agents, or

professional advisors and all or any other third party to whom you make disclosure are aware of the need for secrecy and confidentiality, and will extract a similar written undertaking from them in the vendor's favour. You shall only disclose such matters as are necessary for evaluation and negotiation.

On acceptance of the terms of this document, you shall sign and return it to MacIntyre Hudson.

Agreed to accepted
this   day of

BY:

On behalf of:

(as Potential Purchaser or Investor)

Appendix V

Sample Heads of Agreement

TARGET LIMITED

HEADS OF AGREEMENT

Proposed purchase by Holdings Group Limited
from Mr & Mrs Jones

HEADS OF AGREEMENT

Proposed purchase by Holdings Group Limited ("Holdings) of shares in Target Ltd. ("Target" or "the Company") from Mr. A. Jones and Mrs. B. Jones ("the Vendors")

1. **Status**

   With the exception of paragraphs 10 and 11, which are binding on the parties, these Heads of Agreement are a non-binding statement of intent between the parties and Subject to Contract until substituted by the execution of a formal agreement ("the Agreement") encompassing the contractual and commercial objectives of the parties as expressed herein.

2. **Objective**

   The objective is the purchase by Holdings of the entire issued share capital of Target from the Vendors. Subsequent to the acquisition of Target by Holdings, it is the intention of Holdings to transfer Target to its subsidiary, Trading Limited.

3. **Timetable**

   The parties shall use all reasonable endeavours to enter into the agreement within two months of the date of these Heads of Agreement and to complete the share purchases in accordance with the terms of the Agreement as soon as possible thereafter. Pending completion, the Company shall carry on business in the normal course and shall not enter into any unusual, abnormal or onerous transactions without the prior written consent of Holdings.

4. Price

At completion Holdings will acquire the whole of the issued share capital of Target for an estimated consideration of £5,000,000.

This amount is to be payable as to £4,000,000 at completion in either cash or redeemable loan notes at the discretion of the Vendors.

The remaining amount payable ("Second Tranche") will be paid after the results for the year to 31 December 2011 have been agreed. The Second Tranche will be satisfied by redeemable loan notes.

The redeemable loan notes will be guaranteed by a high street clearing bank.

The Second Tranche will calculated as 5.54 times the Adjusted Pre-Tax Profits for the year ended 31 December 2011, subject to a maximum total consideration of £7.0 million.

The offer price assumes a level of net assets at completion of at least £800,000. Should the actual level be less than that then there will be a £ for £ reduction in the acquisition price. Should the actual level exceed £850,000 there will be a £ for £ increase in the acquisition price.

All monies owed to or by the Vendors by or to the Company will be repaid in full on completion.

5. Management

Until such time as the integration plans (see point 6 below) are put in place, the Company will continue to be managed in the same way as at present. After completion of the Agreement Holdings will nominate three additional board members to represent its interests.

6. Integration Plans

It is intended that the Company will become fully integrated with the other businesses within Trading Limited. The integration will not take place until after 31 December 2011 but planning and preparation for this will be developed as soon as the Agreement has been completed.

7. Conditions Precedent

Finalisation of the Agreement will be dependent upon:

● There being no further shareholders' costs (being management charges, administrative charges, dividends or similar charges) charged to the profit and loss account from the date of this letter to completion of the transaction, other than in the ordinary course of business.

● The satisfactory outcome of legal due diligence, and of an investigation into the title and valuation of the freehold property owned by the Company.

● Holdings and Holdings' financial backers being satisfied with the results of a focused due diligence exercise into the commercial and financial affairs of the Company; and the formal confirmation of Holdings' funding by its financial backers and completion of any legal documentation required to give effect to this funding.

● The Vendors entering into a three-year Employment

Contract with the Company to manage the business and help train their replacements. The compensation to the Vendors shall total £150,000 per annum.

● If required by the Vendors, tax clearances will be obtained in respect of the transaction and the loan notes.

8. Warranties and Indemnities

The Vendors will give normal common form warranties and indemnities, in particular covering issues concerning, accounting and trading matters and taxation.

9. Restrictive Covenants

The Vendors will give whatever undertakings Holdings require that they will not in the future compete with the current business of Target.

10. Exclusivity

Holdings is granted a six week period of exclusivity from the date hereof during which time neither the Vendors nor their advisers will solicit any offer or approach from, or enter into or pursue any negotiations with, any other person or body for that person to acquire Target.

11. Confidentiality

Following the signing of these Heads of Agreement, all parties will – to the extent that they are not already so bound – maintain strict confidentiality over the terms of the same and reveal only such information to their staff and professional advisers as is necessary to achieve a satisfactory conclusion of the transactions hereby contemplated.

12. Definitions

For the purpose of establishing the "Adjusted Pre-Tax Profits" of the Company for the purposes of these Heads of Agreement, the accounts of the Company shall be prepared in accordance with and by the adoption of the accounting standards and policies adopted in the preparation of the audited accounts to 31 December 2010.

The "Adjusted Pre-Tax Profits" of the Company shall be the operating profit of the Company (after charging interest payable and after crediting interest receivable and before deducting any taxation on profits) as disclosed by the audited accounts of the Company after taking account of adjustments for any non-recurring directors' remuneration or any other exceptional costs or revenues of a non-recurring nature and any costs from Holdings group companies not charged on an arms-length basis but otherwise including all costs properly associated with generating the level of profits shown.

13. Costs

Each party hereto shall be responsible for their own costs and expenses incurred by them respectively in relation to implementing the Agreement.

14. Governing Law

The terms set out herein shall be governed by and construed in accordance with English law and each party hereby agrees to submit for all purposes in connection with this matter to the exclusive jurisdiction of the English courts.

Signed ....

duly authorised for and on behalf of
Holdings Group Limited

Signed ....

Mr. A. Jones

Signed ....

Mrs. B. Jones

Dated: ....

Appendix VI

Sample Sale and Purchase Agreement relating to the sale of the whole of the issued share capital of Target Limited

TABLE OF CONTENTS

SCHEDULE 3 CONDITIONS

SCHEDULE 4 COMPLETION
Part 1 - Conduct between exchange and Completion
Part 2 - What the Sellers shall deliver to the Buyer at Completion
Part 3 - Matters for the board meetings at Completion

SCHEDULE 5 WARRANTIES
Part 1 - General Warranties
Part 2 - Tax warranties

SCHEDULE 6 TAX COVENANT

SCHEDULE 7 INTELLECTUAL PROPERTY RIGHTS
Part 1 - Registered Intellectual Property Rights
Part 2 - Material unregistered Intellectual Property Rights
Part 3 - Intellectual Property Rights licensed from third parties
Part 4 - Intellectual Property Rights licensed to third parties

SCHEDULE 8 INFORMATION TECHNOLOGY
Part 1 - Particulars of IT system
Part 2 - Particulars of IT contracts

SCHEDULE 9 PARTICULARS OF PROPERTIES
Part 1 - Freehold Properties
Part 2 - Leasehold Properties

THIS AGREEMENT is dated [DATE]

PARTIES

(1)   The several persons whose names and addresses are set out in Part 1 of Schedule 1 (Sellers).

(2)   [FULL COMPANY NAME] incorporated and registered in England and Wales with company number [NUMBER] whose registered office is at [REGISTERED OFFICE ADDRESS] (Buyer).

BACKGROUND

(A)   The Company has an issued share capital of [SHARE CAPITAL] divided into [NUMBER AND CLASS OF SHARES] of [NOMINAL AMOUNT].

(B)   Further particulars of the Company and of the Subsidiaries at the date of this agreement are set out in Schedule 2.

(C)   The Sellers are the legal and beneficial owners of, or are otherwise able to procure the transfer of, the legal and beneficial title to the number of Sale Shares set out opposite their respective names in Part 1 of Schedule 1 comprising in aggregate the whole of the issued share capital of the Company.

(D)   The Sellers have agreed to sell and the Buyer has agreed to buy the Sale Shares subject to the terms and conditions of this agreement.

AGREED TERMS

1.   **INTERPRETATION**

1.1   The definitions and rules of interpretation in this clause apply in this agreement.

Accounts:	the audited financial statements of the Company and the Subsidiaries as at and to the Accounts Date, comprising the individual accounts of the Company and the Subsidiaries, and in the case of the Company the consolidated group accounts of the Company and Subsidiaries, including in each case the balance sheet, profit and loss account together with the notes on them, the cash flow statement and the auditor's and directors' reports [SPECIFY IF DIFFERENT] (copies of which are attached to the Disclosure Letter).
Accounts Date:	[ACCOUNTS DATE].
Business:	the business of the Company and the Subsidiaries, namely [DEFINITION OF THE BUSINESS CARRIED ON BY THE COMPANY AND THE SUBSIDIARIES].
Business Day:	a day (other than a Saturday, Sunday or public

holiday) when banks in [the City of London] are open for business.

Buyer's Solicitors: [NAME AND ADDRESS].

CAA 2001: the Capital Allowances Act 2001.

Claim and Substantiated Claim:

have the meanings set out respectively in clause 7.

Company: [TARGET NAME], a company incorporated and registered in England and Wales with company number [NUMBER] whose registered office is at [REGISTERED OFFICE ADDRESS] further details of which are set out in Part 1 of Schedule 2.

Completion: completion of the sale and purchase of the Sale Shares in accordance with this agreement.

Completion Date: has the meaning given in clause 5.

Conditions: the conditions set out in Schedule 3.

Connected: in relation to a person, has the meaning given section 1122 of the Corporation Tax Act 2010.

Control: in relation to a body corporate, the power of a person to secure that the affairs of the body corporate are conducted in accordance with the wishes of that person:

(a) by means of the holding of shares, or the possession of voting power, in or in relation to that or any other body corporate, or

(b) by virtue of any powers conferred by the constitutional or corporate documents, or any other document, regulating that or any other body corporate,

and a Change of Control occurs if a person who controls any body corporate ceases to do so or if another person acquires Control of it.

Director: each person who is a director or shadow director of the Company or any of the Subsidiaries, the names of whom are set out in Schedule 2.

Disclosed: fairly [, fully, clearly and accurately] disclosed (with sufficient details to identify the nature and scope of the matter disclosed) in or under the Disclosure Letter.

Disclosure Letter: the letter from the Sellers[' Solicitors] to the

Buyer['s Solicitors] with the same date as this agreement that is described as the disclosure letter, including the bundle of documents attached to it (Disclosure Bundle).

Encumbrance: any interest or equity of any person (including any right to acquire, option or right of pre-emption) or any mortgage, charge, pledge, lien, assignment, hypothecation, security, title retention or any other security agreement or arrangement.

Event: has the meaning given in Schedule 6.

FSMA: the Financial Services and Markets Act 2000.

Group: in relation to a company, that company, its subsidiaries [subsidiary undertakings], any company of which it is a subsidiary (its holding company)[subsidiary undertaking (its parent undertaking)]and any other subsidiaries of any such holding company[subsidiary undertakings of any such parent undertaking], and each company in a group is a member of the group.

Unless the context requires otherwise, the application of the definition of Group to any company at any time will apply to the company as it is at that time.

holding company and subsidiary: mean a "holding company" and "subsidiary" as defined in section 1159 of the Companies Act 2006 [and a company shall be treated, for the purposes only of the membership requirement contained in subsections 1159(1)(b) and (c), as a member of another company even if its shares in that other company are registered in the name of (a) another person (or its nominee), whether by way of security or in connection with the taking of security, or (b) its nominee].

ICTA 1988: the Income and Corporation Taxes Act 1988.

IHTA 1984: the Inheritance Tax Act 1984.

Intellectual Property Rights: has the meaning given in paragraph 20.1 of Part 1 of Schedule 5.

Management Accounts: the unaudited balance sheet and the unaudited consolidated profit and loss account of the Company and the Subsidiaries [(including any notes thereon)] for the period of [NUMBER] months ended [DATE] (a copy of which is attached to the Disclosure Letter).

Pension Scheme: the [NAME OF SCHEME] established with effect from [DATE] and which is registered under Chapter 2 Part 4 of the Finance Act 2004.

Previously-owned Land and Buildings: has the meaning given in paragraph 24.1 of Part 1 of Schedule 5.

Properties: has the meaning given in paragraph 24.1 of Part 1 of Schedule 5.

Purchase Price: the purchase price for the Sale Shares to be paid by the Buyer to the Sellers in accordance with clause 4.

Sale Shares: the [NUMBER AND CLASS OF ISSUED SHARES] of [NOMINAL VALUE OF SALE SHARES] each in the Company, all of which have been issued and are fully paid.

Sellers' Solicitors: [NAME AND ADDRESS].

Subsidiaries: the companies, details of which are set out in Part 2 of Schedule 2.

[subsidiary undertaking and parent undertaking: mean a "subsidiary undertaking" and "parent undertaking" as defined in section 1162 of the Companies Act 2006].

Tax Covenant: the tax covenant as set out in Schedule 6.

Tax or Taxation: has the meaning given in Schedule 6.

Tax Claim: has the meaning given in Schedule 6.

Tax Warranties: the Warranties in Part 2 of Schedule 5.

Taxation Authority: has the meaning given in Schedule 6.

Taxation Statute: has the meaning given in Schedule 6.

TCGA 1992: the Taxation of Chargeable Gains Act 1992.

TMA 1970: the Taxes Management Act 1970.

Transaction: the transaction contemplated by this agreement or any part of that transaction.

VATA 1994: the Value Added Tax Act 1994.

Warranties: the representations and warranties in clause 6 and Schedule 5.

[Warrantors: those persons whose names are set out in Part 2 of Schedule 1.]

1.2 Clause and Schedule headings do not affect the interpretation of this agreement.

1.3 A person includes a natural person, corporate or unincorporated body (whether or not having separate legal personality) and that person's personal representatives, successors or permitted assigns.

1.4 Unless the context otherwise requires, words in the singular include the plural and in the plural include the singular.

1.5 Unless the context otherwise requires, a reference to one gender includes a reference to the other genders.

1.6 Subject to clause 14, a reference to any party shall include that party's personal representatives, successors and permitted assigns.

1.7 A reference to a company shall include any company, corporation or other body corporate , wherever and however incorporated or established.

1.8 A reference to a particular statute, statutory provision or subordinate legislation is a reference to it as it is in force [from time to time OR at the date of this agreement,] taking account of any amendment or re-enactment and includes any statute, statutory provision or subordinate legislation which it amends or re-enacts and subordinate legislation for the time being in force made under it. [Provided that, as between the parties, no such amendment or re-enactment made after the date of this agreement shall apply for the purposes of this agreement to the extent that it would impose any new or extended obligation, liability or restriction on, or otherwise adversely affect the rights of, any party.]

1.9 Writing or written includes faxes but not e-mail.

1.10 Documents in agreed form are documents in the form agreed by the parties or on their behalf and initialled by them or on their behalf for identification.

1.11 A reference in this agreement to other documents referred to in this agreement or similar expression is a reference to the following documents: [SPECIFY ANY RELEVANT DOCUMENTS REFERRED TO, SUCH AS THE DISCLOSURE LETTER].

1.12 References to clauses and schedules are to the clauses and schedules of this agreement, references to paragraphs are to paragraphs of the relevant schedule.

1.13 [Any reference to an English legal term for any action, remedy, method of judicial proceeding, legal document, legal status, court, official or any legal concept or thing shall, in respect of any jurisdiction other than England, be deemed to include a reference to what most nearly approximates to the English legal term in that jurisdiction.]

1.14 Unless otherwise expressly provided, the obligations and liabilities of the Sellers under this agreement are joint and several.

1.15 Reference to this agreement include this agreement as amended or varied in accordance with its terms.

1.16 Any words following the terms including, include, in particular or any similar expression shall be construed as illustrative and shall not limit the sense of the words, description, definition, phrase or term preceding those terms.

2.   CONDITIONS

2.1   Completion of this agreement is subject to:

2.1.1   the Conditions in paragraph 1 to paragraph 5 of Schedule 3 being satisfied or waived by the date and time provided in clause 2.4, and

2.1.2   the Condition in paragraph 6 of Schedule 3 being satisfied up to and including the Completion Date or waived.

2.2   If any of the Conditions are not satisfied or waived by the date and time referred to in clause 2.1 and clause 2.4, this agreement shall cease to have effect immediately after that date and time except for:

2.2.1   the provisions set out in clause 2.3,

2.2.2   any rights or liabilities that have accrued under this agreement, and

2.2.3   [OTHER RELEVANT PROVISIONS].

2.3   The following provisions shall continue to have effect, notwithstanding failure to waive or satisfy the Conditions:

2.3.1   clause 1,

2.3.2   clause 2.2 and this clause 2.3,

2.3.3   clause 12,

2.3.4   clause 15,

2.3.5   clause 16,

2.3.6   clause 17,

2.3.7   clause 18,

2.3.8   clause 25, and

2.3.9   clause 26.

2.4   The Sellers and the Buyer shall use all reasonable endeavours (so far as lies within their respective powers) to procure that the Conditions in paragraph 1 to paragraph 5 of Schedule 3 are satisfied as soon as practicable and in any event no later than:

2.4.1   6.00pm on [DATE], or

2.4.2   at such later time and date as may be agreed in writing by the Sellers and the Buyer.

2.5   The Buyer and the Sellers shall co-operate fully in all actions necessary to procure the satisfaction of the Conditions including, but not limited to, the provision by all parties of all information reasonably necessary to make any notification or filing [that the Buyer deems to be necessary] or as requested by any relevant authority, keeping all parties informed of the progress of any notification or filing and providing such assistance as may reasonably be required.

2.6   The Buyer may, to such extent as it thinks fit and is legally entitled to do so, waive any of the Conditions in paragraphs [PARAGRAPH NUMBERS] of Schedule 3 by written notice to the Sellers.

3. SALE AND PURCHASE AND WAIVER OF PRE-EMPTION RIGHTS

3.1 On the terms of this agreement and subject to the Conditions, with effect from Completion, the Sellers shall sell, and the Buyer shall buy, the Sale Shares with full title guarantee free from all Encumbrances and together with all rights that attach (or may in the future attach) to them including, in particular, the right to receive all dividends and distributions declared, made or paid on or after the date of this agreement.

3.2 Each of the Sellers severally waives any right of pre-emption or other restriction on transfer in respect of the Sale Shares or any of them conferred on him under the articles of association of the Company or otherwise and shall, before Completion, procure the irrevocable waiver of any such right or restriction conferred on any other person who is not a party to this agreement.

3.3 The Buyer is not obliged to complete the purchase of any of the Sale Shares unless the purchase of all the Sale Shares is completed simultaneously.

4. PURCHASE PRICE

4.1 The Purchase Price is £[AMOUNT], payable in cash at Completion to [the Sellers[' Solicitors] in the proportions set out opposite the Sellers' names in Schedule 1.

4.2 The Purchase Price shall be deemed to be reduced by the amount of any payment made to the Buyer:

4.2.1 for a breach of any Warranty, or

4.2.2 under clause 10, or

4.2.3 under the Tax Covenant.

5. COMPLETION

5.1 Completion shall take place on the Completion Date:

5.1.1 at the offices of [NAME OF PARTY] at [TIME], or

5.1.2 at any other place or time as agreed in writing by the Sellers and the Buyer.

5.2 Completion Date means [DATE] but:

5.2.1 if the Conditions in [paragraph 1 to paragraph 5] of Schedule 3 have not been satisfied or waived in accordance with clause 2 on or before that date, means:

5.2.1.1 the second Business Day after they are all satisfied or waived, or

5.2.1.2 any other date agreed in writing by the Sellers and the Buyer, or

5.2.2 if Completion is deferred in accordance with clause 5.6, means the date to which it is deferred.

5.3 The Sellers undertake to the Buyer that the Business shall be conducted in the manner provided in Part 1 of Schedule 4 from the date of this agreement until Completion and give the Buyer the undertakings set out in that Schedule.

5.4 At Completion the Sellers shall:

    5.4.1 deliver or cause to be delivered the documents and evidence set out in Part 2 of Schedule 4,

    5.4.2 procure that a board meeting of the Company and each of the Subsidiaries is held at which the matters identified in Part 3 of Schedule 4 are carried out, and

    5.4.3 deliver any other documents referred to in this agreement as being required to be delivered by them.

5.5 At Completion the Buyer shall:

    5.5.1 pay the Purchase Price by [AGREED METHOD OF PAYMENT] to [the Sellers OR the Sellers' Solicitors (who are irrevocably authorised to receive the same)] and otherwise in accordance with clause 4.1. Payment made in accordance with this clause shall constitute a valid discharge of the Buyer's obligations under clause 3.1,

    5.5.2 [deliver a certified copy of the resolution(s) passed by the shareholders of the Buyer authorising the Transaction, and]

    5.5.3 deliver a certified copy of the resolution adopted by the board of directors of the Buyer authorising the Transaction and the execution and delivery by the officers specified in the resolution of this agreement, and any other documents referred to in this agreement as being required to be delivered by it.

5.6 If the Sellers do not comply with clause 5.4 in any material respect, the Buyer may, without prejudice to any other rights it has:

    5.6.1 proceed to Completion, or

    5.6.2 defer Completion to a date no more than 28 days after the date on which Completion would otherwise have taken place, or

    5.6.3 rescind this agreement.

5.7 The Buyer may defer Completion under clause 5.6 only once, but otherwise this clause 5 applies to a Completion deferred under that clause as it applies to a Completion that has not been deferred.

5.8 As soon as possible after Completion the Sellers shall send to the Buyer (at the Buyer's registered office for the time being) all records, correspondence, documents, files, memoranda and other papers relating to the Company and the Subsidiaries not required to be delivered at Completion and which are not kept at any of the Properties.

6. WARRANTIES

6.1 The Buyer is entering into this agreement on the basis of, and in reliance on, the Warranties.

6.2 The Sellers warrant and represent to the Buyer that each Warranty is true, accurate and not misleading on the date of this agreement except as Disclosed.

6.3 The Warranties are deemed to be repeated on each day up to and including the Completion Date and any reference made to the date of this agreement (whether express or implied) in relation to any Warranty shall be construed, in relation to any such repetition, as a reference to each such day.

6.4 The Sellers shall ensure that the Company and each of the Subsidiaries do not do or omit to do anything which would, at any time before or at Completion, be [materially] inconsistent with any of the Warranties, breach any Warranty or make any Warranty untrue or misleading.

6.5 Without prejudice to the right of the Buyer to claim on any other basis or take advantage of any other remedies available to it, if any Warranty is breached or proves to be untrue or misleading, the Sellers shall pay to the Buyer on demand:

6.5.1 the amount necessary to put the Company and each of the Subsidiaries into the position they would have been in if the Warranty had not been breached or had not been untrue or misleading, and

6.5.2 all costs and expenses (including, without limitation, damages, legal and other professional fees and costs, penalties, expenses and consequential losses whether arising directly or indirectly) incurred by the Buyer, the Company or any of the Subsidiaries as a result of such breach or of the Warranty being untrue or misleading (including a reasonable amount in respect of management time).

A payment made in accordance with the provisions of this clause 6.5 shall include any amount necessary to ensure that, after any Taxation of the payment, the Buyer is left with the same amount it would have had if the payment was not subject to Taxation.

6.6 If at any time before or at Completion the Sellers or any of them become aware that a Warranty has been breached, is untrue or is misleading, or has a reasonable expectation that any of those things might occur, they shall immediately:

6.6.1 notify the Buyer in sufficient detail to enable the Buyer to make an accurate assessment of the situation, and

6.6.2 if requested by the Buyer, use their best endeavours to prevent or remedy the notified occurrence.

6.7 If at any time before or at Completion it becomes apparent that a Warranty has been breached, is untrue or misleading, or that the Sellers have breached any other term of this agreement that is material to the sale of the Sale Shares in either case, the Buyer may (without prejudice to any other rights it may have in relation to the breach):

6.7.1 rescind this agreement by notice to the Sellers, or

6.7.2 proceed to Completion.

6.8 Warranties qualified by the expression so far as the Sellers are aware (or any similar expression) are deemed to be given to the best of the knowledge, information and belief of the Sellers after they have made [due and careful enquiries][due and careful enquiries of [NAMED PERSONS]].

6.9 Each of the Warranties is separate and, unless otherwise specifically provided, is not limited by reference to any other Warranty or any other provision in this agreement.

6.10 Except for the matters Disclosed, no information of which the Buyer and/or its agents and/or advisers has knowledge (actual, constructive or imputed), or which could have been discovered (whether by investigation made by the Buyer or made on its behalf), shall prejudice or prevent any Claim or reduce any amount recoverable thereunder.

6.11 The Sellers agree that any information supplied by the Company or any of the Subsidiaries or by or on behalf of any of the employees, directors, agents or officers of the Company and any of the Subsidiaries (Officers) to the Sellers or their advisers in connection with the Warranties, the information Disclosed in the Disclosure Letter or otherwise shall not constitute a warranty, representation or guarantee as to the accuracy of such information in favour of the Sellers, and the Sellers hereby undertake to the Buyer and to the Company, the Subsidiaries and each Officer that they waive any and all claims which they might otherwise have against any of them in respect of such claims.

7. LIMITATIONS ON CLAIMS

7.1 The definitions and rules of interpretation in this clause apply in this agreement.

Claim:	a claim for breach of any of the Warranties.
Substantiated Claim:	a Claim in respect of which liability is admitted by the party against whom such Claim is brought, or which has been adjudicated on by a court of competent jurisdiction and no right of appeal lies in respect of such adjudication, or the parties are debarred by passage of time or otherwise from making an appeal.

A Claim is connected with another Claim or Substantiated Claim if they all arise out of the occurrence of the same event or relate to the same subject matter.

7.2 This clause limits the liability of the Sellers in relation to any Claim [and any claim under the Tax Covenant].

7.3 The liability of the Sellers for all Substantiated Claims [and all claims under the Tax Covenant] when taken together shall not exceed [AMOUNT].

7.4 The Sellers shall not be liable for a Claim [or a claim under the Tax Covenant] unless:

7.4.1 the amount of a Substantiated Claim, or of a series of connected Substantiated Claims of which that Substantiated Claim is one, exceeds [CANNOT MAKE A CLAIM UNLESS IT IS FOR MORE THAN THIS AMOUNT],

7.4.2 [the amount due in respect of a claim under the Tax Covenant exceeds [CANNOT MAKE A CLAIM UNLESS IT IS FOR MORE THAN THIS AMOUNT], and]

7.4.3 the amount of all Substantiated Claims [and all claims under the Tax Covenant] that are not excluded under clause 7.4.1 [and clause 7.4.2]

when taken together exceeds [SELLERS ARE NOT REQUIRED TO PAY FOR ANY CLAIMS UNTIL THE TOTAL OF ALL QUALIFYING CLAIMS EXCEEDS THIS AMOUNT], in which case the whole amount (and not just the amount by which the limit in this clause 7.4.3 is exceeded) is recoverable by the Buyer.

7.5   The Sellers are not liable for any Claim to the extent that the Claim:

7.5.1   relates to matters Disclosed, or

7.5.2   relates to any matter specifically and fully provided for in the Accounts.

7.6   The Sellers are not liable for a Claim [or a claim under the Tax Covenant] unless the Buyer has given the Sellers notice in writing of the Claim [or the claim under the Tax Covenant], summarising the nature of the Claim [or claim under the Tax Covenant] as far as it is known to the Buyer and the amount claimed:

7.6.1   [in the case of a claim made under the Tax Warranties or the Tax Covenant, within the period of seven years beginning with the Completion Date, and]

7.6.2   in any other case, within the period of [PERIOD] beginning with the Completion Date.

7.7   Nothing in this clause 7 applies to a Claim [or a claim under the Tax Covenant] that arises or is delayed as a result of dishonesty, fraud, wilful misconduct or wilful concealment by the Sellers, their agents or advisers.

7.8   The Sellers shall not plead the Limitation Act 1980 in respect of any claims made under the Tax Warranties or Tax Covenant up to seven years after the Completion Date.

8.   PROPERTY

[INCLUDE HERE ANY SPECIFIC PROVISIONS THAT ARE NEEDED IN RELATION TO PROPERTY].

9.   TAX COVENANT

The provisions of Schedule 6 apply in this agreement.

10.   INDEMNITIES

10.1   The Sellers undertake to indemnify, and to keep indemnified, the Buyer, the Company and the Subsidiaries against all losses or liabilities (including, without limitation, any direct or indirect consequential losses, loss of profit and loss of reputation, damages, claims, demands, proceedings, costs, expenses, penalties, legal and other professional fees and costs) which may be suffered or incurred by any of them and which arise directly or indirectly in connection with the following [disputes OR matters]:

10.1.1   [DESCRIPTION OF CASE OR MATTER IN RESPECT OF WHICH INDEMNITY IS TO BE GIVEN], and

10.1.2   [DESCRIPTION OF CASE OR MATTER IN RESPECT OF WHICH INDEMNITY IS TO BE GIVEN].

10.2   Any payment made in respect of a claim under this clause 10 shall include:

10.2.1   an amount in respect of all costs and expenses incurred by the Buyer or the Company or any of the Subsidiaries in relation to the bringing of the claim (including a reasonable amount in respect of management time), and

10.2.2   any amount necessary to ensure that, after any Taxation of the payment, the Buyer is left with the same amount it would have had if the payment was not subject to Taxation.

11.   RESTRICTIONS ON SELLERS

11.1   Each of the Sellers severally covenants with the Buyer that he shall not:

11.1.1   at any time during the period of [NUMBER] years beginning with the Completion Date[, in any geographic areas in which any business of the Company or any of the Subsidiaries was carried on at the Completion Date OR [SPECIFY LOCATION],] carry on or be employed, engaged or interested in any business which would be in competition with any part of the Business as the Business was carried on at the Completion Date, or

11.1.2   at any time during the period of [NUMBER] years beginning with the Completion Date, deal with any person who is at the Completion Date, or who has been at any time during the period of 12 months immediately preceding that date, a client or customer of the Company or any of the Subsidiaries, or

11.1.3   at any time during the period of [NUMBER] years beginning with the Completion Date, canvass, solicit or otherwise seek the custom of any person who is at the Completion Date, or who has been at any time during the period of 12 months immediately preceding that date, a client or customer of the Company or any of the Subsidiaries, or

11.1.4   at any time during the period of [NUMBER] years beginning with the Completion Date:

11.1.4.1   offer employment to, enter into a contract for the services of, or attempt to entice away from the Company or any of the Subsidiaries, any individual who is at the time of the offer or attempt, and was at the Completion Date, employed or directly or indirectly engaged in an executive or managerial position with the Company or any of the Subsidiaries, or

11.1.4.2   procure or facilitate the making of any such offer or attempt by any other person, or

11.1.5   at any time after Completion, use in the course of any business:

11.1.5.1   the words "[PROHIBITED WORDS]", or

11.1.5.2   any trade or service mark, business or domain name, design or logo which, at Completion, was or had been used by the Company or any of the Subsidiaries, or

11.1.5.3   anything which is, in the reasonable opinion of the Buyer, capable of confusion with such words, mark, name, design or logo, or

11.1.6 at any time during a period of [NUMBER] years beginning with the Completion Date, solicit or entice away from the Company or any of the Subsidiaries any supplier to the Company or any of the Subsidiaries who had supplied goods services to the Company or any of the Subsidiaries at any time during the [NUMBER] months immediately preceding the Completion Date, if that solicitation or enticement causes or would cause such supplier to cease supplying, or materially reduce its supply of, those goods or services to the Company or any of the Subsidiaries.

11.2 The covenants in this clause 11 are intended for the benefit of the Buyer, the Company and the Subsidiaries and apply to actions carried out by the Sellers in any capacity and whether directly or indirectly, on the Sellers' own behalf, on behalf of any other person or jointly with any other person.

11.3 Nothing in this clause 11 prevents the Sellers or any of them from holding for investment purposes only:

11.3.1 any units of any authorised unit trust, or

11.3.2 not more than [PERCENTAGE]% of any class of shares or securities of any company traded on [RELEVANT STOCK EXCHANGES].

11.4 Each of the covenants in this clause 11 is a separate undertaking by each Seller in relation to himself and his interests and shall be enforceable by the Buyer separately and independently of its right to enforce any one or more of the other covenants contained in this clause 11. Each of the covenants in this clause 11 is considered fair and reasonable by the parties. If any restriction is found to be unenforceable, but would be valid if any part of it were deleted or the period or area of application reduced, the restriction shall apply with such modifications as may be necessary to make it valid and enforceable.

11.5 The consideration for the undertakings contained in this clause 11 is included in the Purchase Price.

12. CONFIDENTIALITY AND ANNOUNCEMENTS

12.1 Each of the Sellers severally undertakes to the Buyer to keep confidential the terms of this agreement and all information that they have acquired about the [Company and the Subsidiaries] and the Buyer's Group (as such Group is constituted immediately before Completion) and to use the information only for the purposes contemplated by this agreement.

12.2 The Buyer undertakes to each of the Sellers to keep confidential the terms of this agreement and all information that it has acquired about that Seller [and its Group (as such Group is constituted immediately after Completion)] and to use the information only for the purposes contemplated by this agreement.

12.3 [Each of the Sellers severally undertakes to each of the other Sellers to keep confidential the terms of this agreement and all information that they have acquired about that Seller [or its Group (as such Group is constituted immediately after Completion)] and to use the information only for the purposes contemplated by this agreement.]

12.4 The Buyer does not have to keep confidential or restrict its use of information about the Company and the Subsidiaries after Completion.

12.5   Each party to this agreement does not have to keep confidential or to restrict its use of:

12.5.1   information that is or becomes public knowledge other than as a direct or indirect result of a breach of this agreement, or

12.5.2   information that it receives from a source not connected with the party to whom the duty of confidence is owed that it has acquired free from any obligation of confidence to any other person.

12.6   Any party may disclose any information that it is otherwise required to keep confidential under this clause 12:

12.6.1   to such professional advisers, consultants and employees [or officers of its Group] as are reasonably necessary to advise on this agreement, or to facilitate the Transaction, if the disclosing party procures that the people to whom the information is disclosed keep it confidential as if they were that party, or

12.6.2   with the written consent of the other parties, or

12.6.3   [with the written consent of one party, if such information relates only to that party, or]

12.6.4   to confirm that the sale has taken place and the date of the sale (but without otherwise revealing any other terms of sale or making any other announcement),

12.6.5   to the extent that the disclosure is required:

12.6.5.1 by law, or

12.6.5.2 by a regulatory body, Taxation Authority or securities exchange, or

12.6.5.3 to make any filing with, or obtain any authorisation from, a regulatory body, Taxation Authority or securities exchange, or

12.6.5.4 under any arrangements in place under which negotiations relating to terms and conditions of employment are conducted, or

12.6.5.5 to protect the disclosing party's interest in any legal proceedings,

but shall use reasonable endeavours to consult the other parties and to take into account any reasonable requests they may have in relation to the disclosure before making it.

12.7   Each party shall supply any other party with any information about itself[, its Group] or this agreement as such other party may reasonably require for the purposes of satisfying the requirements of a law, regulatory body or securities exchange to which such other party is subject.

13.   **FURTHER ASSURANCE**

The Sellers shall (at their expense) promptly execute and deliver all such documents, and do all such things, as the Buyer may [reasonably] require from time to time for the purpose of giving full effect to the provisions of this agreement.

14.   ASSIGNMENT

14.1   Except as provided otherwise in this agreement, no party may assign, or grant any Encumbrance or security interest over, any of its rights under this agreement or any document referred to in it.

14.2   Each party that has rights under this agreement is acting on its own behalf.

14.3   The Buyer may assign its rights, but not its obligations, under this agreement (or any document referred to in this agreement) to any member of its Group or to any person to whom it transfers the Sale Shares.

14.4   If there is an assignment:

14.4.1   the Sellers may discharge their obligations under this agreement to the assignor until they receive notice of the assignment, and

14.4.2   the assignee may enforce this agreement as if it were a party to it, but the Buyer shall remain liable for any obligations under this agreement.

15.   WHOLE AGREEMENT

15.1   This agreement, and any documents referred to in it, constitute the whole agreement between the parties and supersede any arrangements, understanding or previous agreement between them relating to the subject matter they cover.

15.2   Nothing in this clause 15 operates to limit or exclude any liability for fraud.

16.   VARIATION AND WAIVER

16.1   Any variation of this agreement shall be in writing and signed by or on behalf of the parties.

16.2   Any waiver of any right under this agreement is only effective if it is in writing and it applies only to the party to whom the waiver is addressed and to the circumstances for which it is given, and shall not prevent the party who has given the waiver from subsequently relying on the provision it has waived.

16.3   A party that waives a right in relation to one party, or takes or fails to take any action against that party, does not affect its rights in relation to any other party.

16.4   No failure to exercise or delay in exercising any right or remedy provided under this agreement or by law constitutes a waiver of such right or remedy or shall prevent any future exercise in whole or in part thereof.

16.5   No single or partial exercise of any right or remedy under this agreement shall preclude or restrict the further exercise of any such right or remedy.

16.6   Unless specifically provided otherwise, rights arising under this agreement are cumulative and do not exclude rights provided by law.

17.   COSTS

17.1   Unless otherwise provided, all costs in connection with the negotiation, preparation, execution and performance of this agreement, and any documents referred to in it, shall be borne by the party that incurred the costs.

17.2 The Sellers shall indemnify the Buyer against all costs and expenses incurred by the Buyer in investigating the affairs of the Company's Group and in the negotiation, preparation and performance of this agreement if:

17.2.1 the Buyer rescinds or terminates this agreement, or

17.2.2 Completion does not take place because [STATE RELEVANT CONDITIONS] have not been satisfied in accordance with clause 2.

18. NOTICE

18.1 A notice given under this agreement:

18.1.1 shall be in writing in the English language (or be accompanied by a properly prepared translation into English),

18.1.2 shall be sent for the attention of the person, and to the address or fax number, specified in this clause 18 (or such other address, fax number or person as each party may notify to the others in accordance with the provisions of this clause 18), and

18.1.3 shall be:

18.1.3.1 delivered personally, or

18.1.3.2 sent by fax, or

18.1.3.3 sent by pre-paid first-class post or recorded delivery, or

18.1.3.4 (if the notice is to be served by post outside the country from which it is sent) sent by airmail.

18.2 Any notice to be given to or by all of the Sellers under this agreement is deemed to have been properly given if it is given to or by the Sellers' representative named in clause 18.3. Any notice required to be given to or by some only of the Sellers shall be given to or by the Sellers concerned (and in the case of a notice to the Sellers) at their address or fax number as set out in Schedule 1.

18.3 The addresses for service of notice are:

18.3.1 [SELLERS' REPRESENTATIVE]

18.3.1.1 name:

18.3.1.2 address:

18.3.1.3 for the attention of:

18.3.1.4 fax number:

18.3.2 [BUYER]

18.3.2.1 address:

18.3.2.2 for the attention of:

18.3.2.3 fax number:

18.4 A notice is deemed to have been received:

18.4.1 if delivered personally, at the time of delivery, or

18.4.2 in the case of fax, at the time of transmission, or

18.4.3   in the case of pre-paid first class post or recorded delivery, [NUMBER] Business Days from the date of posting, or

18.4.4   in the case of airmail,[NUMBER] Business Days from the date of posting, or

18.4.5   if deemed receipt under the previous paragraphs of this clause 18.4 is not within business hours (meaning 9.00 am to 5.30 pm Monday to Friday on a day that is not a public holiday in the place of receipt), when business next starts in the place of receipt.

18.5   To prove service, it is sufficient to prove that the notice was transmitted by fax to the fax number of the party or, in the case of post, that the envelope containing the notice was properly addressed and posted.

19.   INTEREST ON LATE PAYMENT

19.1   Where a sum is required to be paid under this agreement (other than under the Tax Covenant) but is not paid before or on the date the parties agreed, the party due to pay the sum shall also pay interest on that sum for the period beginning with that date and ending with the date the sum is paid (and the period shall continue after as well as before judgment).

19.2   The rate of interest shall be [PERCENTAGE]% per annum above the base lending rate for the time being of [FULL NAME OF BANK]. Interest shall accrue on a daily basis and be compounded quarterly.

19.3   This clause 19 is without prejudice to any claim for interest under the law.

20.   SEVERANCE

20.1   If any provision of this agreement (or part of a provision) is found by any court or administrative body of competent jurisdiction to be invalid, unenforceable or illegal, the other provisions shall remain in force.

20.2   If any invalid, unenforceable or illegal provision would be valid, enforceable or legal if some part of it were deleted, the provision shall apply with whatever modification is necessary to give effect to the commercial intention of the parties.

21.   AGREEMENT SURVIVES COMPLETION

This agreement (other than obligations that have already been fully performed) remains in full force after Completion.

22.   THIRD PARTY RIGHTS

22.1   Subject to clause 22.2, this agreement and the documents referred to in it are made for the benefit of the parties and their successors and permitted assigns and are not intended to benefit, or be enforceable by, anyone else.

22.2   The following provisions are intended to benefit future buyers of the Sale Shares from the Buyer and, where they are identified in the relevant clauses, the Company and the Subsidiaries and shall be enforceable by them to the fullest extent permitted by law:

22.2.1   clause 6 and Schedule 5, subject to clause 7,

22.2.2   clause 9 and Schedule 6,

22.2.3   clause 10,

22.2.4   clause 11,

22.2.5   clause 12, and

22.2.6   clause 19.

22.3   Each of the parties represents to the others that their respective rights to terminate, rescind or agree any amendment, variation, waiver or settlement under this agreement are not subject to the consent of any person that is not a party to this agreement.

23.   SUCCESSORS

The rights and obligations of the Sellers and the Buyer under this agreement shall continue for the benefit of, and shall be binding on, their respective successors and assigns.

24.   COUNTERPARTS

This agreement may be executed in any number of counterparts, each of which is an original and which together have the same effect as if each party had signed the same document.

25.   LANGUAGE

If this agreement is translated into any language other than English, the English language text shall prevail.

26.   GOVERNING LAW AND JURISDICTION

26.1   This agreement and any disputes or claims arising out of or in connection with its subject matter or formation (including non-contractual disputes or claims) shall governed by and construed in accordance with the law of England.

26.2   The parties irrevocably agree that the courts of England have exclusive jurisdiction to settle any dispute or claim that arises out of or in connection with this agreement or its subject matter or formation (including non-contractual disputes or claims).

This agreement has been entered into on the date stated at the beginning of it.

SCHEDULE 1

PARTICULARS OF SELLERS [AND WARRANTORS]

Part 1 - Particulars of Sellers and apportionment of Purchase Price

Seller's name, address and fax number	Number of sale shares	Cash consideration	Proportion of Purchase Price

Part 2 - Particulars of [Warrantors]

SCHEDULE 2

PARTICULARS OF THE COMPANY AND THE SUBSIDIARIES

Part 1 - The Company

Name:	
Registration number:	
Registered office:	
[Maximum amount of shares that may be allotted under the articles of association of the Company Amount: £[TOTAL AMOUNT] Divided into: [NUMBER AND CLASS OF SHARES]]	
Issued Share Capital Amount: £[TOTAL AMOUNT OF ISSUED CAPITAL] Divided into: [NUMBER AND CLASS OF SHARES]	
Registered shareholders (and number of Sale Shares held):	
Beneficial owners of Sale Shares (if different) and number of Sale Shares beneficially owned:	
Directors and shadow directors:	
Secretary:	
Auditor	
Registered charges	

Part 2 - The Subsidiaries

Name:	
Registration number:	
Registered office:	
[Maximum amount of shares that may be allotted under the articles of association of the Company Amount: £[TOTAL AMOUNT] Divided into: [NUMBER AND CLASS OF SHARES]]	
Issued Share Capital Amount: £[TOTAL AMOUNT OF ISSUED CAPITAL] Divided into: [NUMBER AND CLASS OF SHARES]	
Registered shareholders (and number of Sale Shares held):	
Beneficial owners of Sale Shares (if different) and number of Sale Shares beneficially owned:	
Directors and shadow directors:	
Secretary:	
Auditor	
Registered charges	

[REPEAT FOR EACH SUBSIDIARY]

SCHEDULE 3

CONDITIONS

1. The despatch by the Buyer to its shareholders of a circular in the agreed form (Circular) and the passing at a general meeting of the Buyer of resolutions in the form set out in the Circular.

2. Where the Buyer is satisfied (whether or not as a result of receiving confirmation to this effect from the European Commission) that the Transaction does not constitute a concentration having a Community dimension within the meaning of Council Regulation (EEC) No. 139/2004 as amended [or any subsequent legislation], then:

   2.1 the Buyer being satisfied (whether or not as a result of receiving confirmation from the Office of Fair Trading) that the Transaction does not constitute a relevant merger situation within the meaning of Part 3 of the Enterprise Act 2002, or

   2.2 the Buyer receiving confirmation in terms satisfactory to it that the Transaction will not be referred to the Competition Commission for further investigation in accordance with Part 3 of the Enterprise Act 2002, or

   2.3 [the Buyer receiving confirmation in terms satisfactory to it that the Transaction will not be referred to the Competition Commission for further investigation on the condition that the Buyer gives specified undertakings to the Office of Fair Trading in accordance with Part 3 of the Enterprise Act 2002 and the terms of those undertakings are in all respects satisfactory to the Buyer, or]

   2.4 [following a reference, the Competition Commission finding that the Transaction is not expected to result in a substantial lessening of competition within any market in the UK for goods or services, or]

   2.5 [following a reference, the Competition Commission finding that the Transaction may be expected to result in a substantial lessening of competition within any market in the UK for goods or services, but that the acceptance of specified undertakings by the Buyer would have the effect of remedying, mitigating or preventing that lessening of competition and the terms of such undertakings being in all respects acceptable to the Buyer.]

3. Where the Transaction constitutes a concentration with a Community dimension within the meaning of Council Regulation (EEC) No. 139/2004 as amended [or any subsequent legislation], then:

   3.1 the Buyer receiving confirmation from the European Commission in terms satisfactory to it that, despite the Transaction constituting such a concentration, the European Commission has decided not to oppose the concentration and has declared it compatible with the Internal Market[, and OR or]

   3.2 [the Buyer, having been told by the European Commission that the Transaction (or any part of it) has been referred to the government, regulatory body or competition authority of any EU member state, receiving confirmation in terms satisfactory to it from that government, regulatory body or competition authority that the Transaction has been approved in accordance with the relevant national legislation of that EU member state, or]

3.3   [the Buyer receiving confirmation from the European Commission in terms satisfactory to it that, despite opening proceedings in relation to the Transaction, the Commission has declared it to be compatible with the Internal Market, or]

3.4   [the Buyer receiving confirmation from the European Commission that the Transaction will be declared to be compatible with the Internal Market[, and proceedings will not be initiated OR whether before or after initiating proceedings,] on the condition that the Buyer gives certain specified undertakings to the European Commission and the terms of those undertakings being in all respects satisfactory to the Buyer.]

4.   [The Buyer receiving confirmation in terms satisfactory to it that the Transaction has been approved and no objections have been raised by:

4.1   [LIST ANY OTHER RELEVANT NATIONAL COMPETITION AUTHORITIES AND NATIONAL MERGER CONTROL RULES IN ANY OTHER COUNTRIES WHERE THE TRANSACTION IS TO BE NOTIFIED FOR CLEARANCE.]]

5.   The following consents, authorisations or similar clearances being granted in terms satisfactory to the Buyer. All those which:

5.1   are required by any government, regulatory body or authority for Completion, or

5.2   are, in the reasonable opinion of the Buyer, necessary or desirable for Completion.

6.   No person:

6.1   having commenced, or threatened to commence, any proceedings or investigation for the purpose of prohibiting or otherwise challenging or interfering with the Transaction, or

6.2   having taken or threatened to take any action as a result of, or in anticipation of, the Transaction that would be materially inconsistent with any of the Warranties, or

6.3   having enacted or proposed any legislation (including any subordinate legislation) which would prohibit, materially restrict or materially delay the implementation of the Transaction or the operations of the Company or any of the Subsidiaries.

SCHEDULE 4

COMPLETION

Part 1 - Conduct between exchange and Completion

1. The Sellers shall procure that the Business shall be conducted in the manner provided in this Part of this Schedule 4 from the date of this agreement to Completion.

2. The Company and the Subsidiaries shall carry on business in the normal course.

3. The Company and each of the Subsidiaries shall not:

    3.1   dispose of any material assets used or required for the operation of its business, or

    3.2   allot or agree to allot any shares or other securities or repurchase, redeem or agree to repurchase or redeem any of the shares, or

    3.3   pass any resolution, or

    3.4   enter into, modify or agree to terminate any Material Contract (as defined in paragraph 13 of Part 1 of Schedule 5, or

    3.5   incur any capital expenditure on any individual item in excess of £[AMOUNT], or

    3.6   borrow any sum in excess of [£[AMOUNT] OR the amounts borrowed in the ordinary course of business and available to it at the date of this agreement], or

    3.7   enter into any lease, lease-hire or hire-purchase agreement or agreement for payment on deferred terms, or

    3.8   pay any dividend or make any other distribution of its assets, or

    3.9   make, or agree to make, material alterations to the terms of employment (including benefits) of any of its directors, officers or employees, or

    3.10 provide or agree to provide any non-contractual benefit to any director, officer, employee or their dependants, or

    3.11 dismiss any of its employees or employ or engage (or offer to employ or engage) any person, or

    3.12 create any Encumbrance over any of its assets or its undertaking, or

    3.13 institute, settle or agree to settle any legal proceedings relating to its business, except debt collection in the normal course of business, or

    3.14 grant, modify, agree to terminate or permit the lapse of any Intellectual Property Rights or enter into any agreement relating to any such rights, or

    3.15 pay any management charge to the Sellers, or

    3.16 incur any liability to the Sellers, other than trading liabilities incurred in the normal course of business, or

3.17   enter into any (or modify any subsisting) agreement with any trade union or any agreement that relates to any works council, or

3.18   vary the terms on which it holds any of the Properties or settle any rent review, or

3.19   make any material change to the accounting procedures or principles by reference to which its accounts are drawn up.

4.   The Company or any of the Subsidiaries may do anything falling within paragraph 3 of Part 1 of this Schedule 4 if the Buyer has given prior written consent.

5.   The Company and each of the Subsidiaries shall maintain in force insurance policies:

5.1   that have limits of indemnity at least equal to, and

5.2   the other terms of which are no less favourable than,

those policies of insurance maintained by the Company or, in relation to one of the Subsidiaries, by that Subsidiary on the date of this agreement.

6.   The Sellers shall use their best endeavours to maintain the trade and trade connections of the Company and the Subsidiaries.

7.   The Sellers shall give to the Buyer as soon as possible full details of any material change in the business, financial position or assets of the Company or any of the Subsidiaries.

8.   The Sellers shall not:

8.1   induce, or attempt to induce, any of the employees of the Company or of any of the Subsidiaries, whether directly or indirectly, to terminate their employment before the Completion Date, or

8.2   incur any liabilities to the Company or any of the Subsidiaries, other than trading liabilities incurred in the normal course of business.

9.   No amendment, other than an amendment made solely to comply with legislative requirements, shall be made to any agreements or arrangements for the payment of pensions or other benefits on retirement:

9.1   to present or former directors, officers or employees of the Company or any of the Subsidiaries, or

9.2   to the dependants of any of those people.

10.   The Sellers shall, at the Buyer's request and the Sellers' expense, provide the Buyer with such information or documents as it may reasonably require relating to the terms of employment or any other matter concerning any Employee, Worker, body of employees or their representatives in the period prior to the Completion Date.

11.   The Sellers shall, at their own expense and subject to their obligations under the Data Protection Act 1998, give such assistance as the Buyer may reasonably require to contest any claim by anyone employed or engaged by the Company prior to the Completion Date or their representatives resulting from or in connection with this agreement.

Part 2 - What the Sellers shall deliver to the Buyer at Completion

1. At Completion, the Sellers shall deliver, or cause to be delivered, to the Buyer the following:

   1.1 transfers of the Sale Shares executed by the registered holders in favour of the Buyer [or its nominees],

   1.2 the share certificates for the Sale Shares in the names of the registered holders or an indemnity in the agreed form for any lost certificates,

   1.3 the waivers, consents and other documents required to enable the Buyer [and its nominees] to be registered as the holder[s] of the Sale Shares,

   1.4 an irrevocable power of attorney in agreed form given by the Sellers in favour of the Buyer [or its nominees] to enable the beneficiary (or its proxies) to exercise all voting and other rights attaching to the Sale Shares before the transfer of the Sale Shares is registered in the register of members,

   1.5 the original of any power of attorney under which any document to be delivered to the Buyer under this paragraph 1 has been executed,

   1.6 certificates in respect of all issued shares in the capital of each of the Subsidiaries and transfers in favour of any person the Buyer directs and of all shares in any Subsidiary held by a nominee for the Company or another Subsidiary,

   1.7 in relation to the Company and each of the Subsidiaries, the statutory registers and minute books (written up to the time of Completion), the common seal, certificate of incorporation and any certificates of incorporation on change of name,

   1.8 the written resignation, executed as a deed and in the agreed form, of the directors [and secretaries] of the Company and each of the Subsidiaries from their offices and employment with the Company or Subsidiary, except for the following persons who are not resigning:

      1.8.1 [NAME OF DIRECTOR WHO IS NOT RESIGNING], and

      1.8.2 [NAME OF DIRECTOR WHO IS NOT RESIGNING],

   1.9 the written resignation of the auditors of the Company and of each of the Subsidiaries (as the case may be), accompanied in each case by:

      1.9.1 a statement in accordance with section 519 of the Companies Act 2006 that there are no circumstances connected with the auditors' resignation which should be brought to the notice of the members or creditors of the Company or of the Subsidiary, and

      1.9.2 a written assurance that the resignation and statement have been, or will be, deposited at the registered office of the Company or Subsidiary in accordance with section 519 of the Companies Act 2006,

   1.10 [the resignations, in the appropriate form, of those trustees of the

[NAME OF PENSION FUND] pension fund that the Buyer requires to resign],

1.11   signed copies of special resolutions of the Company [and any relevant subsidiary] in a form appropriate for filing at Companies House to:

    1.11.1   change the name of the Company to [NEW NAME OF COMPANY],

    1.11.2   [change the name of [NAME OF SUBSIDIARY] to [NEW NAME OF SUBSIDIARY],]

    1.11.3   adopt new articles of association of the Company in the form the Buyer requires, and

    1.11.4   [adopt new articles of association of [NAME OF SUBSIDIARY] in the form the Buyer requires,]

1.12   a copy of the new articles of association of the Company and the Subsidiaries appropriate for filing at Companies House,

1.13   a certified copy of the minutes of the board meetings held pursuant to Part 3 of Schedule 4,

1.14   in relation to the Company and each of the Subsidiaries:

    1.14.1   statements from each bank at which any of those companies has an account, giving the balance of each account at the close of business on the last Business Day before Completion,

    1.14.2   all cheque books in current use and written confirmation that no cheques have been written since those statements were prepared,

    1.14.3   details of their cash book balances, and

    1.14.4   reconciliation statements reconciling the cash book balances and the cheque books with the bank statements delivered,

1.15   all title deeds and other documents relating to the Properties,

1.16   evidence, in agreed form, that any indebtedness or other liability of the kind described in paragraph 14 of Part 1 of Schedule 5 has been discharged,

1.17   evidence, in agreed form, that the Company and the Subsidiaries have been discharged from any responsibility for the indebtedness, or for the default in the performance of any obligation, of any other person, and

1.18   all charges, mortgages, debentures and guarantees to which the Company or any of the Subsidiaries is a party [and, in relation to each such instrument and any covenants connected with it:

    1.18.1   a sealed discharge or release in the agreed form, and

    1.18.2   if applicable, a sworn and completed Form MG02 (statement of satisfaction in full or in part of mortgage or charge).]

Part 3 - Matters for the board meetings at Completion

1. The Sellers shall cause a board meeting of the Company and each of the Subsidiaries to be held at Completion at which the following matters shall take place.

    1.1 a resolution to register the transfer of the Sale Shares shall be passed at such board meeting of the Company, subject to the transfers being stamped at the cost of the Buyer,

    1.2 all directors[, secretaries] and auditors of the Company and the Subsidiaries shall resign from their offices and employment with the Company and the Subsidiaries with effect from the end of the relevant board meeting, except for the following persons:

        1.2.1 [NAME OFFICERS WHO ARE NOT RESIGNING],

    1.3 compromise agreements complying with the requirements of section 203(1) of the Employment Rights Act 1996 shall be entered into between [COMPANY OR ONE OF the Subsidiaries] and [NAME OF OTHER PARTY],

    1.4 service agreements in the agreed form shall be entered into between the following persons [NAME OF PERSON] and [NAME OF EMPLOYING COMPANY],

    1.5 [the trustees of the [NAME OF TARGET'S PENSION FUND] pension fund required to resign by the Buyer shall do so,]

    1.6 the persons the Buyer nominates shall be appointed as directors [and secretary] of the Company and of each of the Subsidiaries (but not exceeding any maximum number of directors contained in the relevant company's articles of association), and the appointments shall take effect at the end of the board meeting,

    1.7 [NAME OF NEW AUDITORS] shall be appointed as the auditors of the Company and each of the Subsidiaries with effect from the end of the relevant board meeting,

    1.8 all the existing instructions and authorities to bankers shall be revoked and replaced with new instructions and authorities to those banks in the form the Buyer requires,

    1.9 the address of the registered office of the Company and of each of the Subsidiaries shall be changed to the address required by the Buyer, and

    1.10 the accounting reference date of the Company and of each of the Subsidiaries shall be changed to the date required by the Buyer.

SCHEDULE 5

WARRANTIES

Part 1 - General Warranties

1.   POWER TO SELL THE COMPANY

1.1.   The Sellers have all requisite power and authority to enter into and perform this agreement in accordance with its terms and the other documents referred to in it.

1.2.   This agreement and the other documents referred to in it constitute (or shall constitute when executed) valid, legal and binding obligations on the Sellers in the terms of the agreement and such other documents.

1.3.   Compliance with the terms of this agreement and the documents referred to in it shall not breach or constitute a default under any of the following:

1.3.1.   any agreement or instrument to which any Seller is a party or by which any Seller is bound, or

1.3.2.   any order, judgment, decree or other restriction applicable to any Seller.

2.   SHARES IN THE COMPANY AND THE SUBSIDIARIES

2.1.   The Sale Shares constitute the whole of the allotted and issued share capital of the Company and are fully paid.

2.2.   The Sellers are the legal and beneficial owners of the Sale Shares.

2.3.   Part 2 of Schedule 2 lists all the Subsidiaries of the Company at the date of this agreement and sets out particulars of their allotted and issued share capital.

2.4.   The Company is the sole legal and beneficial owner of the whole allotted and issued share capital of each of the Subsidiaries.

2.5.   The issued shares of the Subsidiaries are fully paid up.

2.6.   The Sale Shares and the issued shares of the Subsidiaries are free from all Encumbrances.

2.7.   No right has been granted to any person to require the Company or any of the Subsidiaries to issue any share capital and no Encumbrance has been created in favour of any person affecting any unissued shares or debentures or other unissued securities of the Company or any of the Subsidiaries.

2.8.   No commitment has been given to create an Encumbrance affecting the Sale Shares or the issued shares of the Subsidiaries (or any unissued shares or debentures or other unissued securities of the Company or any of the Subsidiaries) or for any of them to issue any share capital and no person has claimed any rights in connection with any of those things.

2.9.   Neither the Company nor any of the Subsidiaries:

2.9.1.   holds or beneficially owns, or has agreed to acquire, any securities of any corporation other than its own Subsidiaries, or

2.9.2. is or has agreed to become a member of any partnership or other unincorporated association, joint venture or consortium (other than recognised trade associations), or

2.9.3. has, outside its country of incorporation, any branch or permanent establishment, or

2.9.4. has allotted or issued any securities that are convertible into shares.

2.10. Neither the Company nor any of the Subsidiaries has at any time:

2.10.1. purchased, redeemed or repaid any of its own share capital, or

2.10.2. [given any financial assistance in contravention of any applicable law or regulation.]

2.11. All dividends or distributions declared, made or paid by the Company and the Subsidiaries have been declared, made or paid in accordance with its memorandum, articles of association, all applicable laws and regulations and any agreements or arrangements made with any third party regulating the payment of dividends and distributions.

3. CONSTITUTIONAL AND CORPORATE DOCUMENTS

3.1. The copies of the memorandum and articles of association or other constitutional and corporate documents of the Company and the Subsidiaries Disclosed to the Buyer or its advisers are true, accurate and complete in all respects and copies of all the resolutions and agreements required to be annexed to or incorporated in those documents by the law applicable are annexed or incorporated.

3.2. All statutory books and registers of the Company and the Subsidiaries have been properly kept and no notice or allegation that any of them is incorrect or should be rectified has been received.

3.3. All returns, particulars, resolutions and other documents that the Company or any of the Subsidiaries is required by law to file with or deliver to any authority in any jurisdiction (including, in particular, the Registrar of Companies in England and Wales) have been correctly made up and filed or, as the case may be, delivered.

4. INFORMATION

4.1. All information contained in the Disclosure Letter [and all information provided by the Sellers and their advisers to the Buyer and its advisers in the course of negotiations] is complete, accurate and not misleading.

4.2. The particulars relating to the Company and the Subsidiaries in this agreement are true and accurate and not misleading.

4.3. There is no information that has not been Disclosed which, if Disclosed, might reasonably affect the willingness of the Buyer to buy the Sale Shares on the terms of this agreement.

5. COMPLIANCE WITH LAWS

The Company and each of the Subsidiaries has at all times conducted its business in accordance with all applicable laws and regulations.

6.   LICENCES AND CONSENTS

6.1.   The Company and each of the Subsidiaries has all necessary licences, consents, permits and authorities necessary to carry on its business in the places and in the manner in which its business is now carried on, all of which are valid and subsisting.

6.2.   There is no reason why any of those licences, consents, permits and authorities should be suspended, cancelled, revoked or not renewed on the same terms.

7.   INSURANCE

7.1.   The insurance policies maintained by or on behalf of the Company and the Subsidiaries provide full indemnity cover against all losses and liabilities, including business interruption and other risks that are normally insured against by a person carrying on the same type of business as the Company and the Subsidiaries.

7.2.   The particulars of those insurance policies set out in the Disclosure Letter are accurate and not misleading.

7.3.   There are no material outstanding claims under, or in respect of the validity of, any of those insurance policies and, so far as the Sellers are aware, there are no circumstances likely to give rise to any claim under any of those insurance policies.

7.4.   All the insurance policies are in full force and effect, are not void or voidable, nothing has been done or not done which could make any of them void or voidable and Completion will not terminate, or entitle any insurer to terminate, any such policy.

8.   POWER OF ATTORNEY

8.1.   There are no powers of attorney in force given by the Company or any of the Subsidiaries.

8.2.   No person, as agent or otherwise, is entitled or authorised to bind or commit the Company or any of the Subsidiaries to any obligation not in the ordinary course of the Company's or any Subsidiary's business.

8.3.   The Disclosure Letter sets out details of all persons who have authority to bind the Company and the Subsidiaries in the ordinary course of business.

9.   DISPUTES AND INVESTIGATIONS

9.1.   Neither the Company nor any of the Subsidiaries nor any person for whom the Company or any of the Subsidiaries is vicariously liable:

9.1.1.   is engaged in any litigation, administrative, mediation or arbitration proceedings or other proceedings or hearings before any statutory or governmental body, department, board or agency (except for debt collection in the normal course of business), or

9.1.2.   is the subject of any investigation, inquiry or enforcement proceedings by any governmental, administrative or regulatory body.

9.2.   No director of the Company or any of the Subsidiaries is, to the extent that it relates to the business of the Company or the Subsidiaries, engaged in or subject to any of the matters mentioned in paragraph 9.1 of Schedule 5.

9.3.   No such proceedings, investigation or inquiry as are mentioned in paragraph 9.1 and paragraph 9.2 of Schedule 5 have been threatened or are pending and there are no circumstances likely to give rise to any such proceedings.

9.4.   The Company and the Subsidiaries are not affected by any existing or pending judgments or rulings and have not given any undertakings arising from legal proceedings to a court, governmental agency, regulator or third party.

10.   DEFECTIVE PRODUCTS AND SERVICES

10.1.   Neither the Company nor any of the Subsidiaries has manufactured or sold any products which were, at the time they were manufactured or sold, faulty or defective or did not comply with:

10.1.1.   warranties or representations expressly made or implied by or on behalf of the Company or any relevant Subsidiary, or

10.1.2.   all laws, regulations, standards and requirements applicable to the products.

10.2.   No proceedings have been started, are pending or have been threatened against the Company or any of the Subsidiaries in which it is claimed that any products manufactured or sold by the company concerned are defective, not appropriate for their intended use or have caused bodily injury or material damage to any person or property when applied or used as intended.

10.3.   No proceedings have been started and there are no outstanding liabilities or claims pending or threatened against the Company or any of the Subsidiaries in respect of any services supplied by the Company or any of the Subsidiaries for which the Company or any of the Subsidiaries is or may become liable and no dispute exists between the Company or any of the Subsidiaries and any of their respective customers or clients.

11.   CUSTOMERS AND SUPPLIERS

11.1.   In the 12 months ending with the date of this agreement, neither the business of the Company nor of any of the Subsidiaries has been materially affected in an adverse manner as a result of any one or more of the following things happening to the Company or any of the Subsidiaries:

11.1.1.   the loss of any of its customers or suppliers, or

11.1.2.   a reduction in trade with its customers or in the extent to which it is supplied by any of its suppliers, or

11.1.3.   a change in the terms on which it trades with or is supplied by any of its customers or suppliers.

11.2.   No one or more of the things mentioned in paragraph 11.1 of Schedule 5 is likely to happen to the extent that the business of the Company or the business of any of the Subsidiaries will be materially affected in an adverse manner.

12. COMPETITION

12.1. The definition in this paragraph applies in this agreement.

Competition Law: the national and directly effective legislation of any jurisdiction which governs the conduct of companies or individuals in relation to restrictive or other anti-competitive agreements or practices (including, but not limited to, cartels, pricing, resale pricing, market sharing, bid rigging, terms of trading, purchase or supply and joint ventures), dominant or monopoly market positions (whether held individually or collectively) and the control of acquisitions or mergers.

12.2. Neither the Company nor any of the Subsidiaries is engaged in any agreement, arrangement, practice or conduct which amounts to an infringement of the Competition Law of any jurisdiction in which the Company or any the Subsidiaries conduct business and no Director is engaged in any activity which would be an offence or infringement under any such Competition Law.

12.3. Neither the Company nor any of the Subsidiaries is the subject of any investigation, inquiry or proceedings by any relevant government body, agency or authority in connection with any actual or alleged infringement of the Competition Law of any jurisdiction in which the Company or any of the Subsidiaries conducts business.

12.4. No such investigation, inquiry or proceedings as mentioned in paragraph 12.3 of Schedule 5 have been threatened or are pending and there are no circumstances likely to give rise to any such investigation, inquiry or proceedings.

12.5. Neither the Company nor any of the Subsidiaries is affected by any existing or pending decisions, judgments, orders or rulings of any relevant government body, agency or authority responsible for enforcing the Competition Law of any jurisdiction and neither the Company nor any of the Subsidiaries have given any undertakings or commitments to such bodies which affect the conduct of the Business.

12.6. Neither the Company nor any of the Subsidiaries is in receipt of any payment, guarantee, financial assistance or other aid from the government or any state body which was not, but should have been, notified to the European Commission under Article 88 of the EC Treaty or Article 108 of the Treaty on the Functioning of the European Union for a decision declaring such aid to be compatible with the Internal Market.

13. CONTRACTS

13.1. The definition in this paragraph applies in this agreement.

Material Contract: an agreement or arrangement to which the Company or any of the Subsidiaries is a party or is bound by and which is of material importance to the business, profits or assets of the Company or any of the Subsidiaries.

13.2. Except for the agreements and arrangements Disclosed, neither the Company nor any of the Subsidiaries is a party to or subject to any agreement or arrangement which:

13.2.1. is a Material Contract, or

13.2.2. is of an unusual or exceptional nature, or

13.2.3. is not in the ordinary and usual course of business of the Company or any of the Subsidiaries, or

13.2.4. may be terminated as a result of any Change of Control of the Company or any of the Subsidiaries, or

13.2.5. restricts the freedom of the Company or any of the Subsidiaries to carry on the whole or any part of its business in any part of the world in such manner as it thinks fit, or

13.2.6. involves agency or distributorship, or

13.2.7. involves partnership, joint venture, consortium, joint development, shareholders' or similar arrangements, or

13.2.8. is incapable of complete performance in accordance with its terms within six months after the date on which it was entered into, or

13.2.9. cannot be readily fulfilled or performed by the Company or the relevant Subsidiary on time and without undue or unusual expenditure of money and effort, or

13.2.10. involves or is likely to involve an aggregate consideration payable by or to the Company or any of the Subsidiaries in excess of £[AMOUNT], or

13.2.11. requires the Company or any of the Subsidiaries to pay any commission, finders' fee, royalty or the like, or

13.2.12. is for the supply of goods and/or services by or to the Company or any of the Subsidiaries on terms under which retrospective or future discounts, price reductions or other financial incentives are given, or

13.2.13. is not on arm's-length terms, or

13.2.14. [provides for payments or other dealings in or calculated by reference to the euro or which will otherwise be affected by the changes arising from European Monetary Union.]

13.3. Each Material Contract is in full force and effect and binding on the parties to it. Neither the Company nor any of the Subsidiaries have defaulted under or breached a Material Contract and:

13.3.1. no other party to a Material Contract has defaulted under or breached such a contract, and

13.3.2. no such default or breach by the Company, any of the Subsidiaries or any other party is likely or has been threatened.

13.4. No notice of termination of a Material Contract has been received or served by the Company or any of the Subsidiaries and there are no grounds for determination, rescission, avoidance, repudiation or a material change in the terms of any such contract.

13.5. [There are no agreements or arrangements to which the Company or any of the Subsidiaries is subject that involve obligations or liabilities that ought reasonably to be made known to the Buyer.]

14. TRANSACTIONS WITH SELLERS

14.1. There is no outstanding indebtedness or other liability (actual or contingent) and no outstanding contract, commitment or arrangement between the Company and any of the following, or between any of the Subsidiaries and any of the following:

14.1.1. any of the Sellers or any person Connected with any of the Sellers, or

14.1.2. any director of a member of the Company's Group or any person Connected with such a member or director.

14.2. None of the Sellers, nor any person Connected with any of the Sellers is entitled to a claim of any nature against the Company or any of the Subsidiaries, or has assigned to any person the benefit of a claim against the Company or any of those Subsidiaries to which the Seller or a person Connected with such Seller would otherwise be entitled.

15. FINANCE AND GUARANTEES

15.1. Full particulars of all money borrowed by the Company and each of the Subsidiaries (including full particulars of the terms on which such money has been borrowed) have been Disclosed.

15.2. No guarantee, mortgage, charge, pledge, lien, assignment or other security agreement or arrangement has been given by or entered into by the Company or any of the Subsidiaries or any third party in respect of borrowings or other obligations of the Company or the Subsidiaries.

15.3. The total amount borrowed by the Company or any of the Subsidiaries does not exceed any limitations on the borrowing powers contained:

15.3.1. in the memorandum and articles of association of the Company or the relevant Subsidiary, or

15.3.2. in any debenture or other deed or document binding on the Company or relevant Subsidiary.

15.4. Neither the Company nor any of the Subsidiaries has any outstanding loan capital, or has lent any money that has not been repaid, and there are no debts owing to the Company or the Subsidiaries other than debts that have arisen in the normal course of business.

15.5. Neither the Company nor any of the Subsidiaries has:

15.5.1. factored any of its debts or discounted any of its debts or engaged in financing of a type which would not need to be shown or reflected in the Accounts, or

15.5.2. waived any right of set-off it may have against any third party.

15.6. All debts (less any provision for bad and doubtful debts) owing to the Company or any of the Subsidiaries reflected in the Accounts and all debts subsequently recorded in the books of the Company and the Subsidiaries have either been realised prior to the date of this agreement or will, within three months after the date of this agreement, realise in cash their full amount as included in those Accounts or books and none of those debts nor any part of them has been outstanding for more than two months from its due date for payment.

15.7. No indebtedness of the Company or any of the Subsidiaries is due and payable and no security over any of the assets of the Company or any of the Subsidiaries is now enforceable, whether by virtue of the stated maturity date of the indebtedness having been reached or otherwise. Neither the Company nor any of the Subsidiaries has received any notice whose terms have not been fully complied with and/or carried out from any creditor requiring any payment to be made and/or intimating the enforcement of any security which it may hold over the assets of the Company or the Subsidiaries.

15.8. Neither the Company nor any of the Subsidiaries has given or entered into any guarantee, mortgage, charge, pledge, lien, assignment or other security agreement or arrangement or is responsible for the indebtedness, or for the default in the performance of any obligation, of any other person.

15.9. Neither the Company nor any of the Subsidiaries is subject to any arrangement for receipt or repayment of any grant, subsidy or financial assistance from any government department or other body.

15.10. Particulars of the balances of all the bank accounts of the Company and the Subsidiaries, showing the position as at the day immediately preceding the date of this agreement, have been Disclosed and the Company and the Subsidiaries have no other bank accounts. Since those particulars were given, there have been no payments out of those accounts other than routine payments in the ordinary course of business.

15.11. Having regard to the existing banking and other facilities available to it, the Company and each of the Subsidiaries has sufficient working capital for the purposes of:

15.11.1. continuing to carry on its business in its present form and at its present level of turnover for the next 12 months, and

15.11.2. executing, carrying out and fulfilling in accordance with their respective terms all orders, projects and contractual obligations that have been placed with or undertaken by the Company and each of the Subsidiaries.

15.12. A Change of Control of the Company will not result in:

15.12.1. termination of or material effect on any financial agreement or arrangement to which the Company, or any of the Subsidiaries, is a party or subject, or

15.12.2. any indebtedness of the Company or of any of the Subsidiaries becoming due, or capable of being declared due and payable, prior to its stated maturity.

16.   INSOLVENCY

16.1. Neither the Company nor any of the Subsidiaries:

16.1.1. is insolvent or unable to pay its debts within the meaning of the Insolvency Act 1986 or any other insolvency legislation applicable to the company concerned, and

16.1.2. has stopped paying its debts as they fall due.

16.2. No step has been taken in any applicable jurisdiction to initiate any process by or under which:

16.2.1. the ability of the creditors of the Company, or any of the Subsidiaries, to take any action to enforce their debts is suspended, restricted or prevented, or

16.2.2. some or all of the creditors of the Company or of any of the Subsidiaries accept, by agreement or in pursuance of a court order, an amount less than the sums owing to them in satisfaction of those sums with a view to preventing the dissolution of the Company or any of the Subsidiaries, or

16.2.3. a person is appointed to manage the affairs, business and assets of the Company, or any of the Subsidiaries, on behalf of the Company's or any of the Subsidiaries' creditors, or

16.2.4. the holder of a charge over all or any of the Company's assets or over all or any of the Subsidiaries' assets is appointed to control the business and/or all or any assets of the Company or any of the Subsidiaries.

16.3. In relation to the Company and each of the Subsidiaries:

16.3.1. no administrator has been appointed,

16.3.2. no documents have been filed with the court for the appointment of an administrator, and

16.3.3. no notice of an intention to appoint an administrator has been given by the relevant company, its directors or by a qualifying floating charge holder (as defined in paragraph 14 of Schedule B1 to the Insolvency Act 1986).

16.4. No process has been initiated which could lead to the Company or any of the Subsidiaries being dissolved and its assets being distributed among the relevant company's creditors, shareholders or other contributors.

16.5. No distress, execution or other process has been levied on an asset of the Company or any of the Subsidiaries.

17. ASSETS

17.1. The Company or one of the Subsidiaries is the full legal and beneficial owner of, and has good and marketable title to, all the assets included in the Accounts, any asset acquired since the Accounts Date and all other assets used by the Company or the Subsidiaries except for those disposed of since the Accounts Date in the normal course of business.

17.2. None of the assets shown in the Accounts or acquired by the Company or any of the Subsidiaries since the Accounts Date or used by the Company or any of the Subsidiaries is the subject of any lease, lease-hire agreement, hire-purchase agreement or agreement for payment on deferred terms or is the subject of any licence or factoring arrangement.

17.3.   The Company or the Subsidiaries is in possession and control of all the assets included in the Accounts or acquired since the Accounts Date and all other assets used by the Company and the Subsidiaries, except for those Disclosed as being in the possession of a third party in the normal course of business.

17.4.   None of the assets, undertaking or goodwill of the Company or the Subsidiaries is subject to an Encumbrance, or to any agreement or commitment to create an Encumbrance, and no person has claimed to be entitled to create such an Encumbrance.

17.5.   The assets of the Company and of each of the Subsidiaries comprise all the assets necessary for the continuation of the relevant company's business [in the manner in which such business is carried on at the Accounts Date and as at Completion].

18.   CONDITION OF PLANT AND EQUIPMENT AND STOCK-IN-TRADE

18.1.   The plant, machinery, equipment and vehicles used in connection with the Business:

18.1.1. are in good working order and have been regularly and properly maintained,

18.1.2. are capable and will continue to be capable of doing the work for which they were designed, and

18.1.3. are not surplus to the current or proposed requirements of the Company and the Subsidiaries.

18.2.   The stock-in-trade (including work-in-progress) of the Company and the Subsidiaries is in good condition and is capable of being sold by the Company or relevant Subsidiary in the ordinary course of its business in accordance with its current price list without discount, rebate or allowance to a buyer.

18.3.   The stock-in-trade (including work-in-progress) of the Company and the Subsidiaries is not excessive and is adequate in relation to the current trading requirements of the Company and the Subsidiaries, and none of the stock is obsolete, slow moving, unusable, unmarketable or includes returned goods.

18.4.   [The stock-in-trade of the Company and the Subsidiaries complies fully and will, on sale by the Company or the relevant Subsidiary in the ordinary and usual course of its business, comply fully with all applicable laws, regulations, standards (including British and European Union standards) and specifications agreed with customers.]

19.   ENVIRONMENT AND HEALTH AND SAFETY

19.1.   The definitions in this paragraph apply in this agreement.

CRC:	the CRC Energy Efficiency Scheme established by the CRC Order.
CRC Order:	the CRC Energy Efficiency Scheme Order 2010 (SI 2010/768).
Environment:	the natural and man-made environment, including all or any of the following media,

namely air, water and land (including air within buildings and other material or man-made structures above or below the ground) and any living organisms (including man) or systems supported by those media.

Environmental and Health and Safety Laws:

all applicable laws, statutes, regulations, secondary legislation, bye-laws, common law, directives, treaties and other measures, judgments and decisions of any court or tribunal, codes of practice and guidance notes which are legally binding and in force as at the date of this agreement in so far as they relate to or apply to the Environment or the health and safety of any person.

Environmental and Health and Safety Matters:

all matters relating to:

(a) pollution or contamination of the Environment,

(b) the presence, existence, disposal, release, spillage, deposit, escape, discharge, leak, migration or emission of Hazardous Substances or Waste,

(c) the exposure of any person to any Hazardous Substances or Waste,

(d) the health and safety of any person, including any accidents, injuries, illnesses and diseases,

(e) the creation or existence of any noise, vibration, odour, radiation, common law or statutory nuisance or other adverse impact on the Environment, or

(f) the condition, protection, maintenance, remediation, reinstatement, restoration or replacement of the Environment or any part of it.

Environmental and Health and Safety Permits:

any permits, licences, consents, certificates, registrations, notifications or other authorisations required under any Environmental and Health and Safety Laws for the operation of the Business or in relation to any of the Properties.

Harm:

harm to the Environment, and in the case of man includes offence caused to any of his senses or harm to his property.

Hazardous Substances:

any material, substances or organisms which,

alone or in combination with others, are capable of causing Harm, including radioactive substances and asbestos containing materials.

Undertaking and subsidiary undertaking:
mean, for the purposes of this paragraph 19 only, an "undertaking" and a "subsidiary undertaking" as defined in the CRC Order.

Waste:
any waste, including any by-product of an industrial process and anything which is discarded, disposed of, spoiled, abandoned, unwanted or surplus, irrespective of whether it is capable of being recovered or recycled or has any value.

19.2. The Company and each of the Subsidiaries have obtained and have at all times complied with all Environmental and Health and Safety Permits, all Environmental and Health and Safety Permits are in full force and effect, and there are no facts or circumstances that may lead to the revocation, suspension, variation or non-renewal of any Environmental and Health and Safety Permits.

19.3. The Company and each of the Subsidiaries have at all times complied with all Environmental and Health and Safety Laws and there are no facts or circumstances which may lead to any breach of or liability under any Environmental and Health and Safety Laws.

19.4. All information provided by or on behalf of the Company or any of the Subsidiaries to any relevant enforcement authority, and all records and data required to be maintained by the Company or any of the Subsidiaries under the provisions of any Environmental and Health and Safety Laws are complete and accurate.

19.5. There are no Hazardous Substances at, on or under, nor have any Hazardous Substances been emitted, escaped or migrated from, any of the Properties.

19.6. There are, and have been, no landfills, underground storage tanks or mining operations, uncontained or unlined storage treatment or disposal areas for Hazardous Substances or Waste (whether permitted by Environmental and Health and Safety Laws or otherwise) present or carried out at, on or under any of the Properties or within 200 metres of any of the Properties. There are no polychlorinated biphenyls or asbestos containing materials at, on or under any of the Properties.

19.7. There have been no claims, investigations, prosecutions or other proceedings against or threatened against the Company, any of the Subsidiaries or any of its respective directors, officers or employees in respect of Harm arising from the operation of the Business or occupation of any of the Properties or for any breach or alleged breach of any Environmental and Health and Safety Permits, Environmental and Health and Safety Laws and there are no facts or circumstances which may lead to any such claims, investigations, prosecutions or other proceedings. At no time has the Company or any of the Subsidiaries received any notice, communication or information alleging any liability in relation to any Environmental and Health and Safety Matters or that any works are required.

19.8. Neither the Company nor any of the Subsidiaries have received any enforcement, prohibition, stop, remediation, improvement or any other notice from any enforcement authority, including the Environment Agency, the Health and Safety Executive and the relevant local authority, with regard to any breach or alleged breach of any Environmental and Health and Safety Laws.

19.9. Neither the Company nor any of the Subsidiaries has or is likely to have any actual or potential liability under any Environmental and Health and Safety Laws by reason of it having owned, occupied or used any Previously-owned Land and Buildings.

19.10. The Company and the Subsidiaries have adequate employers' liability and public liability insurance cover in respect of the Business and the Properties. No claims have been made or are contemplated under any such insurance cover.

19.11. Copies of all:

19.11.1. current Environmental and Health and Safety Permits,

19.11.2. environmental and health and safety policy statements,

19.11.3. reports in respect of environmental and health and safety audits, investigations or other assessments,

19.11.4. records of accidents, illnesses and reportable diseases,

19.11.5. assessments of substances hazardous to health,

19.11.6. correspondence between the Company or any of the Subsidiaries and any relevant enforcement authority, and

19.11.7. copies or details of all waste disposal contracts relating to the Business or any of the Properties have been disclosed to the Buyer and all such statements, reports, investigations, assessments, records, correspondence and other information are complete and accurate and are not misleading.

19.12. Neither the Company nor any of the Subsidiaries have given or received any warranties or indemnities in respect of (or have otherwise attempted to apportion) any liabilities, duties or obligations that arise under Environmental and Health and Safety Laws.

19.13. [The Company and each of the Subsidiaries have complied with the requirements of the:

19.13.1. Producer Responsibility (Packaging Waste) Regulations 2007,

19.13.2. Waste Electrical and Electronic Equipment Regulations 2006, and

19.13.3. Restriction of the Use of Certain Hazardous Substances in Electrical and Electronic Equipment Regulations 2008,

and full details of those requirements have been disclosed to the buyer.]

Paragraphs 19.14 to 19.17 may be used where the Company is not required to participate in the CRC.

19.14. [All information provided by or on behalf of the Sellers and/or any of their advisers to the Buyer and/or any of its advisers:

19.14.1. regarding the supply of electricity to the Company, the Subsidiaries and any undertakings that were subsidiary undertakings of the Company on 31 December 2008, and

19.14.2. otherwise in connection with the CRC,

is, at the date of this agreement, complete, accurate and not misleading.

19.15. The Company and its subsidiary undertakings as at 31 December 2008, did not meet the qualification criteria set out in the CRC Order during the calendar year 2008 or any part of that year.

19.16. The Company and the Subsidiaries are not required to participate in the current phase of the CRC.

19.17. The Company and each of the Subsidiaries [are not required to provide any information to the administrator of the CRC under article 62 of the CRC Order OR have, to the extent required, fully complied with the requirements of article 62 of the CRC Order].]

Paragraphs 19.18 to 19.21 may be used where the Company is required to participate in the CRC.

19.18. [All information provided by or on behalf of the Sellers and/or any of their advisers to the Buyer and/or any of its advisers:

19.18.1. regarding the supply of energy to the Company, the Subsidiaries and any undertakings that were subsidiary undertakings of the Company on 31 December 2008 or at any time during the current phase of the CRC, and

19.18.2. otherwise in connection with the CRC,

is, at the date of this agreement, complete, accurate and not misleading.

19.19. The Company and its subsidiary undertakings as at 31 December 2008, met the qualification criteria set out in the CRC Order during the calendar year 2008 or any part of that year.

19.20. The Company and the Subsidiaries are required to participate in the current phase of the CRC.

19.21. The Company has registered for the current phase of the CRC in accordance with the provisions of the CRC Order.]

20. INTELLECTUAL PROPERTY

20.1. The definition in this paragraph applies in this agreement.

Intellectual Property Rights: patents, rights to inventions, copyright and related rights, [moral rights,] trade marks [and service marks], trade names and domain names, [rights in get-up,] rights to goodwill or to sue for passing off [or unfair competition,] rights in designs, rights in computer software, database rights, rights in confidential information (including know-how [and trade secrets]) and any other intellectual property rights, in each case whether registered or unregistered and including all applications (or rights to apply) for, and renewals or extensions of, such rights and all similar or equivalent rights or forms of protection which subsist or will subsist now or in the future in any part of the world.

20.2. Complete and accurate particulars are set out in Part 1 and Part 2 of Schedule 7 respectively of all registered Intellectual Property Rights (including applications for such rights) and material unregistered Intellectual Property Rights owned, used or held for use by the Company and the Subsidiaries.

20.3. Complete and accurate particulars are set out in Part 3 and Part 4 of Schedule 7 respectively of all licences, agreements, authorisations and permission (in whatever form and whether express or implied) under which:

20.3.1. the Company or any of the Subsidiaries uses or exploits Intellectual Property Rights owned by any third party, or

20.3.2. the Company or any of the Subsidiaries has licensed or agreed to license Intellectual Property Rights to, or otherwise permitted the use of any Intellectual Property Rights by, any third party.

20.4. Except as set out in Part 3 and Part 4 of Schedule 7, the Company or the relevant specified Subsidiary is the sole legal and beneficial owner of (or applicant for) the Intellectual Property Rights set out in Part 1 and Part 2 of Schedule 7, free from all Encumbrances.

20.5. The Company and the Subsidiaries do not require any Intellectual Property Rights other than those set out in Part 1 and Part 2 of Schedule 7 in order to carry on their respective activities.

20.6. The Intellectual Property Rights set out in Part 1 and Part 2 of Schedule 7 are valid, subsisting and enforceable and nothing has been done or not been done as a result of which any of them has ceased or might cease to be valid, subsisting or enforceable. In particular:

20.6.1. all application and renewal fees and other steps required for the maintenance or protection of such rights have been paid on time or taken,

20.6.2. all confidential information (including know-how and trade secrets) owned or used by the Company or the Subsidiaries has been kept confidential and has not been disclosed to third parties (other than parties who have signed written confidentiality undertakings in respect of such information, details of which refer to undertakings are set out in the Disclosure Letter),

20.6.3. no mark, trade name or domain name identical or similar to any such rights has been registered, or is being used by any person in the same or a similar business to that of the Company or any of the Subsidiaries, in any country in which the Company or any Subsidiary has registered or is using that mark, trade name or domain name, and

20.6.4. there are and have been no claims, challenges, disputes or proceedings, pending or threatened, in relation to the ownership, validity or use of such rights.

20.7. Nothing is due to be done within 30 days of Completion the omission of which would jeopardise the maintenance or prosecution of any of the Intellectual Property Rights owned or used by the Company or any of the Subsidiaries which are registered or the subject of an application for registration.

20.8. There has been no infringement by any third party of any Intellectual Property Right set out in Part 1 and Part 2 of Schedule 7, nor any third party breach of confidence, passing off or actionable act of unfair competition in relation to the business and assets of the Company or any of the Subsidiaries, and no such infringement, breach of confidence, passing off or actionable act of unfair competition is current or anticipated.

20.9. The agreements and licences set out in Part 3 and Part 4 of Schedule 7:

20.9.1. are valid and binding,

20.9.2. have not been the subject of any breach or default by any party or of any event which, with the giving of notice or lapse of time, would constitute a default,

20.9.3. are not the subject of any claim, dispute or proceeding, pending or threatened, and

20.9.4. have, where required, been duly recorded or registered.

20.10. A Change of Control of the Company or any of the Subsidiaries will not result in the termination of, or have a material affect on, any of the Intellectual Property Rights set out in Schedule 7.

20.11. The activities of the Company, each of the Subsidiaries and of any licensee of Intellectual Property Rights granted by the Company or any of the Subsidiaries:

20.11.1. have not infringed, do not infringe and are not likely to infringe the Intellectual Property Rights of any third party, or

20.11.2. have not constituted, do not constitute and are not likely to constitute any breach of confidence, passing off or actionable act of unfair competition, or

20.11.3. have not given and do not give rise to any obligation to pay any royalty, fee, compensation or any other sum whatsoever.

21. **INFORMATION TECHNOLOGY**

21.1. The definitions in this paragraph apply in this agreement.

IT System: all computer hardware (including network and telecommunications equipment) and

	software (including associated preparatory materials, user manuals and other related documentation) owned, used, leased or licensed by or to the Company or any of the Subsidiaries.
IT Contracts:	all arrangements and agreements under which any third party (including, without limitation, any source code deposit agents) provides any element of, or services relating to, the IT System, including leasing, hire-purchase, licensing, maintenance and services agreements.

21.2.   Complete and accurate particulars of the IT System and all IT Contracts are set out in Part 1 and Part 2 of Schedule 8.

21.3.   Save to the extent provided in the IT Contracts, the Company and the Subsidiaries are the owners of the IT System free from Encumbrances. The Company and the Subsidiaries have obtained all necessary rights from third parties to enable them to make exclusive and unrestricted use of the IT System.

21.4.   The IT Contracts are valid and binding and no act or omission has occurred which would, if necessary with the giving of notice or lapse of time, constitute a breach of any such contract.

21.5.   There are and have been no claims, disputes or proceedings arising or threatened under any IT Contracts.

21.6.   None of the IT Contracts is liable to be terminated or otherwise materially affected by a Change of Control of the Company and/or the Subsidiaries, and the Sellers have no reason to believe that any IT Contracts will not be renewed on the same or substantially the same terms when they expire.

21.7.   The Company and the Subsidiaries have possession or control of the source code of all software in the IT System, or have the right to gain access to such code under the terms of source code deposit agreements with the owners of the rights in the relevant software and reputable deposit agents (particulars of which are set out in Part 2 of Schedule 8).

21.8.   The elements of the IT System:

21.8.1. are functioning properly and in accordance with all applicable specifications,

21.8.2. are not defective in any respect and have not been materially defective or materially failed to function during the last [three] years,

21.8.3. do not contain any software virus and have not within the last [12 months] been infected by any software virus or accessed by any unauthorised person,

21.8.4. have sufficient capacity and performance to meet the current and foreseeable business requirements of the Company and the Subsidiaries,

21.8.5. include sufficient user information to enable reasonably skilled personnel in the field to use and operate the IT System without the need for further assistance, and

21.8.6. have been satisfactorily and regularly maintained and the IT System has the benefit of appropriate maintenance and support agreements, complete and accurate particulars of which are set out in Part 2 of Schedule 8.

21.9. The Company and the Subsidiaries have implemented appropriate procedures, (including in relation to off-site working where applicable) for ensuring the security of the IT System and the confidentiality and integrity of all data stored in it.

21.10. The Company and the Subsidiaries have in place a disaster recovery plan which is fully documented and would enable the business of the Company and the Subsidiaries to continue if there were significant damage to or destruction of some or all of the IT System. A copy of the plan is attached to the Disclosure Letter.

21.11. The performance and functionality of the IT System (and any other equipment and systems owned or used by the Company or the Subsidiaries which depend on date-programmed control devices) has not been affected and will be unaffected by any changes in dates (past, present or future). In particular:

21.11.1. no value for a current date has caused or will cause any interruption in operation,

21.11.2. date-based functionality has behaved and will behave consistently for all dates,

21.11.3. in all interfaces and data storage, the century in any date is and will be specified either explicitly or by unambiguous algorithms or inferencing rules, and

21.11.4. all leap years (including 2004 and 2008) will be recognised as such.

21.12. The IT System is capable of:

21.12.1. performing its functions in multiple currencies, including the euro,

21.12.2. satisfying all applicable legal requirements relating to the euro, including the conversion and rounding rules in EC Regulation 1103/97,

21.12.3. displaying and printing the generally accepted symbols for the euro and any other currency, and

21.12.4. processing the generally accepted codes for the euro and any other currency.

22. DATA PROTECTION

22.1. The Company and the Subsidiaries have notified registrable particulars under the Data Protection Act 1998 of all personal data held by them and:

22.1.1. have renewed such notifications and have notified any changes occurring in between such notifications as required by that Act,

22.1.2. have paid all fees payable in respect of such notifications,

22.1.3. the contents of such notifications (copies of which are attached to the Disclosure Letter) are complete and accurate, and

22.1.4. there has been no unauthorised disclosure of personal data outside the terms of such notifications.

22.2.   No personal data have been transferred outside the European Economic Area.

22.3.   The Company and the Subsidiaries have:

22.3.1.   complied in all respects with the Data Protection Act 1984 and the Data Protection Act 1998 (including in relation to any manual data in respect of which the transitional exemptions under Schedule 8 of the Data Protection Act 1998 have now expired),

22.3.2.   satisfied any requests for access to personal data subject to paragraph 22.3.1 of Schedule 5,

22.3.3.   established the procedures necessary to ensure continued compliance with such legislation, and

22.3.4.   complied with the requirements of the seventh principle of the Data Protection Act 1998 in respect of any processing of data carried out by a data processor on behalf of the Company or any of the Subsidiaries, including by entering into a written contract with the data processor confirming that the data processor will only act on the instructions of the Company or the relevant Subsidiary, and requiring the data processor to comply with obligations relating to security measures equivalent to those imposed on the Company or the relevant Subsidiary by the seventh principle as mentioned above.

22.4.   Neither the Company nor any of the Subsidiaries has received any:

22.4.1.   notice or complaint under the Data Protection Act 1998 alleging non-compliance with that Act (including any information or enforcement notice, or any transfer prohibition notice), or

22.4.2.   claim for compensation for loss or unauthorised disclosure of data, or

22.4.3.   notification of an application for rectification or erasure of personal data,

and neither the Company nor any of its Subsidaries is aware of any circumstances which may give rise to the giving of any such notice or the making of any such notification.

22.5.   The Company and the Subsidiaries have complied with their obligations under the Privacy and Electronic Communications (EC Directive) Regulations 2003 in respect of the use of electronic communications (including e-mail, text messaging, fax machines, automated calling systems and non-automated telephone calls) for direct marketing purposes.

23.   EMPLOYMENT

23.1.   The definitions in this paragraph apply in this agreement.

Employment Legislation: legislation applying in England and Wales affecting contractual or other relations between employers and their employees or workers including, but not limited to, any legislation and any amendment, extension or re-enactment of such legislation and any claim arising under European treaty provisions or directives enforceable against the Company or any of the Subsidiaries by any Employee or Worker.

Employee: any person employed by the Company or any of the Subsidiaries under a contract of employment.

Worker: any person who personally performs work for the Company or any of the Subsidiaries but who is not in business on their own account or in a client/customer relationship.

23.2. The name of each Director is set out in Schedule 2.

23.3. The Disclosure Letter includes anonymised details of all Employees and Workers of the Company and the Subsidiaries, the particulars of each Employee and Worker and the principal terms of their contract including:

23.3.1. the company which employs or engages them,

23.3.2. their current remuneration (including any benefits and privileges that the Company or the relevant Subsidiary provides or is bound to provide to them or their dependants, whether now or in the future),

23.3.3. the commencement date of each contract and, if an Employee, the date on which continuous service began,

23.3.4. the length of notice necessary to terminate each contract or, if a fixed term, the expiry date of the fixed term and details of any previous renewals,

23.3.5. the type of contract (whether full or part-time or other),

23.3.6. their date of birth,

23.3.7. any country in which the Employee or Worker works or performs services and/or is paid, if the Employee or Worker works or is paid outside England and Wales, and

23.3.8. the law governing the contract, if the Employee or Worker works or is paid outside England and Wales.

23.4. The Disclosure Letter includes anonymised details of all persons who are not Workers and who are providing services to the Company or any of the Subsidiaries under an agreement which is not a contract of employment with the Company or the relevant Subsidiary (including, in particular, where the individual acts as a consultant or is on secondment from an employer which is not a member of the Company's Group) and the particulars of the terms on which the individual provides services, including:

23.4.1. the company which engages them,

23.4.2. the remuneration of each individual (including any benefits and privileges that the Company or any of the Subsidiaries provides or is bound to provide) to them or their dependants, whether now or in the future,

23.4.3. the length of notice necessary to terminate each agreement or, if a fixed term, the expiry date of the fixed term and details of any previous renewals.

23.4.4. any country in which the individual provides services, if the individual provides services wholly or mainly outside England and Wales, and

23.4.5. the law governing the agreement, if the individual provides services wholly or mainly outside England and Wales.

23.5. The Disclosure Letter includes anonymised details of all Employees and Workers of the Company and the Subsidiaries who are on secondment, maternity, paternity, adoption or other leave or who are absent due to ill-health or for any other reason.

23.6. No notice to terminate the contract of employment of any Employee or Worker of the Company or any Subsidiary (whether given by the relevant employer or by the Employee or Worker) is pending, outstanding or threatened and no dispute under any Employment Legislation or otherwise is outstanding between:

23.6.1. the Company or any Subsidiary and any of its or their current or former Employees relating to their employment, its termination or any reference given by the Company or any Subsidiary regarding them, or

23.6.2. the Company or any Subsidiary and any of its or their current or former Workers relating to their contract, its termination or any reference given by the Company or any Subsidiary regarding them.

23.7. No questionnaire has been served on the Company or any of the Subsidiaries by an Employee or Worker under any Employment Legislation which remains unanswered in full or in part.

23.8. Every Employee or Worker of the Company and any Subsidiary who requires permission to work in the United Kingdom has current and appropriate permission to work in the United Kingdom.

23.9. No offer of employment or engagement has been made by the Company or by any of the Subsidiaries that has not yet been accepted, or which has been accepted but where the employment or engagement has not yet started.

23.10. The acquisition of the Sale Shares by the Buyer and compliance with the terms of this agreement will not entitle any Directors, officers or [senior] Employees of the Company or any of the Subsidiaries to terminate their employment or receive any payment or other benefit.

23.11. All contracts between the Company or any Subsidiary and its or their Employees and Workers are terminable at any time on not more than three months' notice without compensation (other than for unfair dismissal or a statutory redundancy payment) or any liability on the part of the Company or any Subsidiary other than wages, commission or pension.

23.12. All contracts between the Company or the Subsidiaries and their Directors, Employees or Workers comply with any relevant requirements of section 188 of the Companies Act 2006.

23.13. Neither the Company nor any of the Subsidiaries is a party to, bound by or proposing to introduce in respect of any of its Directors or Employees any redundancy payment scheme in addition to statutory redundancy pay, nor is there any agreed procedure for redundancy selection.

23.14. Neither the Company nor any of the Subsidiaries is a party to, bound by or proposing to introduce in respect of any of its Directors, Employees or Workers any incentive scheme (including, without limitation, any share option arrangement, commission, profit sharing or bonus scheme).

23.15. [There are no incentive schemes or other incentive arrangements (including, without limitation, any share option arrangement, commission, profit sharing or bonus scheme) established by any member of the Company's Group or any shareholder of the Company in which the Company or any of the Subsidiaries or any of their respective Directors, Employees or Workers participates.]

23.16. Neither the Company nor any of the Subsidiaries has incurred any actual or contingent liability in connection with any termination of employment of its Employees (including redundancy payments) or for failure to comply with any order for the reinstatement or re-engagement of any Employee.

23.17. Neither the Company nor any of the Subsidiaries has incurred any liability for failure to provide information or to consult with Employees under any Employment Legislation.

23.18. Neither the Company nor any of the Subsidiaries has made or agreed to make a payment or provided or agreed to provide a benefit to a present or former Director or officer, Employee or Worker or to their dependants in connection with the actual or proposed termination or suspension of employment or variation of an employment contract.

23.19. Neither the Company nor any of the Subsidiaries is involved in any material industrial or trade dispute or negotiation regarding a claim with any trade union, group or organisation of employees or their representatives representing Employees or Workers and there is nothing likely to give rise to such a dispute or claim.

23.20. No subject access requests made to the Company or any of the Subsidiaries pursuant to the Data Protection Act 1998 by Employees or Workers are outstanding and the Company and the Subsidiaries have complied with the provisions of the Data Protection Act 1998 in respect of all personal data held or processed by them relating to their Employees, Workers, and former Employees and Workers.

23.21. Neither the Company nor any Subsidiary has in the last [12] months altered and they shall not alter (whether to take effect prior to, on or after the Completion Date) any of the terms of employment or engagement of any of the Employees or Workers (without the prior written consent of the Buyer).

23.22. Neither the Company nor any Subsidiary has or will transfer or agree to transfer any Employee or Worker from working for the Company or any Subsidiary, induce any Employee or Worker to resign their employment with the Company or any Subsidiary without the prior written consent of the Buyer.

23.23. There are no sums owing to or from any Employee or Worker other than reimbursement of expenses, wages for the current salary period and holiday pay for the current holiday year.

23.24. Neither the Company nor any Subsidiary has offered, promised or agreed to any future variation in the contract of any Employee or Worker.

23.25. The Disclosure Letter includes:

23.25.1. anonymised copies of all contracts, handbooks, policies and other documents which apply to any of the Employees and Workers, and

23.25.2. copies of all agreements or arrangements with any trade union, employee representative or body of employees or their representatives (whether binding or not) and details of any unwritten agreements or arrangements which may affect any Employee or Worker.

23.26. In respect of each Employee and Worker, the Company and the Subsidiaries have:

23.26.1. performed all obligations and duties they are required to perform (and settled all outstanding claims), whether or not legally binding and whether arising under contract, statute, at common law or in equity or under any treaties including the EC Treaty or the Treaty on the Functioning of the European Union or laws of the European Union or otherwise,

23.26.2. complied with the terms of any relevant agreement or arrangement with any trade union, employee representative or body of employees or their representatives (whether binding or not), and

23.26.3. maintained adequate, suitable and up-to-date records.

23.27. No Employee is subject to a current disciplinary warning or procedure.

23.28. No employment related securities or securities options (as defined in Part 7 of the Income Tax (Earnings and Pensions) Act 2003) (without limitation, including shares in the Company and options over them) have been issued, granted or transferred in respect of employment or office with the Company or any Subsidiary.

23.29. There are no securities, options over securities or interests in securities (other than those securities or options referred to in paragraph 23.27 above) in respect of which the Company or any Subsidiary may have to account for income tax or national insurance contributions liabilities (or equivalent obligations in any jurisdiction) of any Director, Employee or Worker.

24. PROPERTY

24.1. The definitions in this paragraph apply in this agreement.

Current Use:	the use identified for each Property as set out in Schedule 9.
Freehold Properties:	the freehold properties set out in Part 1 of Schedule 9 and Freehold Property means any one of them or part or parts of any one of them
Investment Lease:	a lease, underlease or occupational licence identified in Schedule 9 as being one to which a Property is subject, and all documents that are supplemental or collateral to such lease, underlease or occupational licence.

Investment Property:	a Property identified in Schedule 9 as being subject to an Investment Lease.
Lease:	the Lease under which each Leasehold Property is held.
Leasehold Properties:	the Leasehold Properties set out in Part 2 of Schedule 9 and Leasehold Property means any one of them or part or parts of any one of them.
Previously-owned Land and Buildings:	land and buildings that have, at any time before the date of this agreement, been owned (under whatever tenure) and/or occupied and/or used by the Company or any of the Subsidiaries, but which are either no longer owned, occupied or used by the Company or any of the Subsidiaries, or are owned, occupied or used by one of them but pursuant to a different lease, licence, transfer or conveyance.
Planning Legislation:	any primary or secondary legislation from time to time regulating the use or development of land.
Properties:	the Freehold Properties and the Leasehold Properties and Property means any one of them or any part or parts of any one of them.
Statutory Agreement:	an agreement or undertaking entered into under any legislation.
Tenant:	a tenant in whom an Investment Lease is currently vested.

24.2. The particulars of the Properties set out in Schedule 9 are true, complete and accurate.

24.3. The Properties are the only land and buildings owned, used or occupied by the Company and the Subsidiaries.

24.4. Neither the Company nor any of the Subsidiaries has any right of ownership, right of use, option, right of first refusal or contractual obligation to purchase, or any other legal or equitable right, estate or interest in, or affecting, any land or building other than the Properties.

24.5. Neither the Company, nor any company that is or has at any time been a subsidiary of the Company, has any actual or contingent liability in respect of Previously-owned Land and Buildings.

24.6. Neither the Company, nor any company that is or has at any time been a subsidiary of the Company, has given any guarantee or indemnity for any liability relating to any of the Properties, [any of the Investment Leases,] any Previously-owned Land and Buildings or any other land or building.

24.7.   All written replies given by or on behalf of the Sellers, the Company or any Subsidiary in response to any written enquiries raised by or on behalf of the Buyer in relation to the Properties were complete and accurate at the date they were given, and would still be complete and accurate if the replies were instead being given on the Completion Date.

24.8.   The Company, or the Subsidiary identified as the owner of each Property in Schedule 9, is solely legally and beneficially entitled and has a good and marketable title, to it.

24.9.   The Company, or the Subsidiary identified as the owner of each Property in Schedule 9, is in possession and actual occupation of the whole of it on an exclusive basis, and no right of occupation or enjoyment has been acquired or is in the course of being acquired by any third party, and neither the Company nor any Subsidiary has granted, or agreed to grant, any right of occupation or enjoyment in respect of the Properties to any third party.

24.10. [The Sellers have in their possession and control OR The Sellers have, held by the Sellers' Solicitors to the order of the Sellers] and have Disclosed:

24.10.1. copies of all the title deeds and documents necessary to prove good and marketable title to the Properties, and

24.10.2. in relation to each Lease:

24.10.2.1.   evidence of the reversioner's title to the Lease,

24.10.2.2.   all consents required under the Lease,

24.10.2.3.   copies of all assignments of the Lease, and

24.10.2.4.   evidence of the current annual rent payable under the Lease.

24.11. All the documents of title to be delivered to the Buyer on the Completion Date shall be original documents, properly stamped with stamp duty and registered, where required.

24.12. Where title to any of the Properties is not registered at HM Land Registry, there is no caution against first registration of title and no event has occurred in consequence of which a caution against first registration of title could be effected.

24.13. There is no circumstance that could render any transaction affecting the title of the Company, or any of the Subsidiaries, to any of the Properties liable to be set aside under the Insolvency Act 1986.

24.14. There are no insurance policies relating to any issue of title affecting the Properties.

24.15. There are, appurtenant to each of the Properties, all rights and easements necessary for their Current Use and enjoyment (without restriction as to time or otherwise). Access to each of the Properties is over roads adopted by the local authority and maintained at public expense and such roads immediately abut the Properties at each point where access is gained.

24.16. The unexpired residue of the term granted by each Lease [and each Investment Lease] is vested in the Company, or any of its Subsidiaries, and is valid and subsisting against all persons, including any person in whom any superior estate or interest is vested.

24.17.   In relation to each Lease and each Investment Lease, the landlord and each lessee, tenant, licensee or occupier has observed and performed in all material respects all covenants, restrictions, stipulations and other encumbrances and there has not been (expressly or impliedly) any waiver of or acquiescence to any breach of them.

24.18.   In relation to each Lease and each Investment Lease, all principal rent and additional rent and all other sums payable by each lessee, tenant, licensee or occupier under each Lease or Investment Lease (Lease Sums) have been paid as and when they became due and no Lease Sums have been:

24.18.1. set off or withheld, or

24.18.2. commuted, waived or paid in advance of the due date for payment.

24.19.   No collateral assurances, undertakings or concessions have been made by any party to any Lease.

24.20.   No premium or principal rent has been taken or accepted from or agreed with any lessee, tenant, licensee or occupier under any Lease beyond what is legally permitted.

24.21.   Any consents required for the grant of each Lease, and for the assignments of each Lease, have been obtained and placed with the documents of title along with evidence of the registration of grant where required.

24.22.   The Properties (and the proceeds of sale from them) are free from:

24.22.1. any mortgage, debenture, charge (whether legal or equitable and whether fixed or floating), rent charge, lien or other right in the nature of security, and

24.22.2. any agreement for sale, estate contract, option, right of pre-emption or right of first refusal,

and there is no agreement or commitment to give or create any of them.

24.23.   The Properties are not subject to the payment of any outgoings other than non-domestic local business rates and water and sewerage charges (and, in the case of the Leasehold Properties, principal rent, insurance premiums and service charges) and all outgoings have been paid when due and none is disputed.

24.24.   The Properties are not subject to any matters which are [, or (where title to any of the Properties is not registered) would be unregistered interests which override first registration under Schedule 1 to the Land Registration Act 2002 [or unregistered interests which override registered dispositions under Schedule 3 to the Land Registration Act 2002].

24.25.   There are no covenants, restrictions, stipulations, easements, profits à prendre, wayleaves, licences, grants or other encumbrances (whether of a private or public nature, and whether legal or equitable) affecting the Properties which are of an onerous or unusual nature, or affect their value, or which conflict with the Current Use of the Properties.

24.26.   All covenants, restrictions, stipulations and other encumbrances affecting the

Properties have been fully observed and performed and no notice of any alleged breach has been received by the Company (or its predecessors in title) or its Subsidiaries (or their predecessors in title).

24.27. There are no circumstances which (with or without taking other action) would entitle any third party to exercise a right of entry to, or take possession of, all or any part of the Properties, or which would in any other way affect or restrict the continued possession, enjoyment or use of any of the Properties.

24.28. There are no matters which are registered as local land charges or, although not registered, are capable of registration as local land charges.

24.29. The Company and the Subsidiaries have not (nor has anyone on their behalf) expressly or impliedly waived any breach by any person of any covenant, agreement, restriction, stipulation or obligation relating to the Properties or of which the Properties have the benefit.

24.30. All of the Properties, other than the Investment Properties, are actively used by the Company or the Subsidiaries in connection with the Business. The Investment Properties are held by the Company or the Subsidiaries as investments.

24.31. The Current Use of each of the Properties is the permitted use for the purposes of the Planning Legislation. Where applicable, the Current Use of each of the Properties is in accordance with the provisions of the Leases and the Investment Leases.

24.32. All necessary building regulation consents have been obtained in relation to both the Current Use of the Properties and any alterations and improvements to them.

24.33. No claim or liability (contingent or otherwise) under the Planning Legislation in respect of the Properties, or any Statutory Agreement affecting the Properties, is outstanding, nor are the Properties the subject of a notice to treat or a notice of entry, and no notice, order resolution or proposal has been published for the compulsory acquisition, closing, demolition or clearance of the Properties, and the neither the Company nor the Subsidiaries are aware of any matter or circumstances which would lead to any such notice, order, resolution or proposal.

24.34. All planning permissions, orders and regulations issued under the Planning Legislation, and all building regulations, consents and byelaws for the time being in force have been fully complied with in relation to the Properties.

24.35. The Company and the Subsidiaries have complied with all applicable statutory and bye-law requirements and all regulations, rules and delegated legislation, relating to the Properties and their Current Use.

24.36. Each of the Properties is in a good state of repair and condition [and fit for the Current Use].

24.37. There are no development works, redevelopment works or fitting-out works outstanding in respect of any of the Properties.

24.38. None of the Properties has suffered from any of the following:

24.38.1. flooding, or

24.38.2. subsidence, or

24.38.3. heave, or

24.38.4. landslip, or

24.38.5. mining activities, or

24.38.6. structural defects, or

24.38.7. defects in the drains and services from time to time serving the Properties, or

24.38.8. dry rot, wet rot, rising damp or any infestation.

24.39. Neither the Company nor the Subsidiaries have received any adverse report from any engineer, surveyor or other professional relating to any of the Properties and they are not aware of any predecessor in title having done so.

24.40. No notices, complaints or requirements have been issued or made (whether formally or informally) by any competent authority or undertaking exercising statutory or delegated powers in relation to any of the Properties, the Current Use of the Properties or any machinery, plant or equipment in them, and neither the Company nor the Subsidiaries are aware of any matter which could lead to any such notice, complaint or requirement being issued or made.

24.41. There exists no dispute between the Company and the Subsidiaries and the owner or occupier of any other premises adjacent to or neighbouring the Properties and neither the Company nor the Subsidiaries expect, or are aware of, any circumstances that may give rise to any such dispute [after the date of this agreement].

24.42. There is no outstanding application for any consent under any Investment Lease.

24.43. There is no pending rent review under any Investment Lease.

25.   ACCOUNTS

25.1. The Accounts have been prepared in accordance with accounting standards, policies, principles and practices generally accepted in the UK and in accordance with the applicable law and regulation of that jurisdiction.

25.2. The Accounts have been audited by an auditor or firm of accountants qualified to act as auditors in the UK and the auditors' report(s) required to be annexed to the Accounts is unqualified.

25.3. The Accounts:

25.3.1. make proper and adequate provision for all bad and doubtful debts, obsolete or slow-moving stock and for depreciation on fixed assets,

25.3.2. do not overstate the value of current or fixed assets, and

25.3.3. do not understate any liabilities (whether actual or contingent).

25.4. The Accounts give a true and fair view of the state of affairs of the Company and the Subsidiaries (and, in relation to the consolidated accounts, of the Company and the Subsidiaries, and of the Company's Group as a whole) as at the Accounts Date and of the profit or loss of the Company and the Subsidiaries, and of the Company's Group, for the financial year ended on that date.

25.5. The Accounts contain either provision adequate to cover, or full particulars in notes to cover, all Taxation (including deferred Taxation) and other liabilities (whether quantified, contingent, disputed or otherwise) of the Company and the Subsidiaries as at the Accounts Date.

25.6. The Accounts are not affected by any unusual or non-recurring items or any other factor that would make the financial position and results shown by the Accounts unusual or misleading in any material respect.

25.7. The Accounts have been filed and laid before the Company in general meeting in accordance with the requirements of all applicable laws and regulations.

25.8. The Accounts have been prepared on a basis consistent with the audited accounts of, as the case may be, the Company, the Subsidiaries or the consolidated accounts of the Company and the Subsidiaries for the [two] prior accounting periods without any change in accounting policies used.

25.9. The Management Accounts have been prepared on a basis consistent with that employed in preparing the Accounts and fairly represent the [assets and liabilities and the profits and losses OR income and expenditure] of the Company and the Subsidiaries as at and to the date for which they have been prepared.

26. FINANCIAL AND OTHER RECORDS

26.1. All financial and other records of the Company and of each of the Subsidiaries:

26.1.1. have been properly prepared and maintained,

26.1.2. constitute an accurate record of all matters required by law to appear in them,

26.1.3. do not contain any material inaccuracies or discrepancies, and

26.1.4. are in the possession of the Company or the Subsidiary to which they relate.

26.2. No notice has been received or allegation made that any of those records are incorrect or should be rectified.

26.3. All statutory records, including accounting records, required to be kept or filed by the Company or any of the Subsidiaries have been properly kept or filed and comply with the requirements of all applicable laws and regulations.

26.4. All deeds and documents belonging to the Company are in the possession of the Company and those belonging to the Subsidiaries are in the possession of the Subsidiary to which they belong.

27. CHANGES SINCE THE ACCOUNTS DATE

27.1 Since the Accounts Date:

27.1.1. the Company and each of the Subsidiaries has conducted its business in the normal course and as a going concern,

27.1.2. there has been no material adverse change in the turnover, financial position or prospects of the Company or any of the Subsidiaries,

27.1.3. neither the Company nor any of the Subsidiaries has issued or agreed to issue any share or loan capital,

27.1.4. no dividend or other distribution of profits or assets has been, or agreed to be, declared, made or paid by the Company or any of the Subsidiaries,

27.1.5. neither the Company nor any of the Subsidiaries has borrowed or raised any money or taken any form of financial security and no capital expenditure has been incurred on any individual item by the Company or any of the Subsidiaries in excess of £[AMOUNT] and neither the Company nor any of the Subsidiaries has acquired, invested or disposed of (or agreed to acquire, invest or dispose of) any individual item in excess of £[AMOUNT],

27.1.6. no shareholder resolutions of the Company or any of the Subsidiaries have been passed other than as routine business at the annual general meeting,

27.1.7. there has been no abnormal increase or reduction of stock-in-trade,

27.1.8. none of the stock-in-trade reflected in the Accounts has realised an amount less than the value placed in it in the Accounts, and

27.1.9. neither the Company nor any of the Subsidiaries has offered price reductions, discounts or allowances on sales of stock-in-trade, or sold stock-in-trade at less than cost price.

28.   EFFECT OF SALE ON SALE SHARES

28.1   Neither the acquisition of the Sale Shares by the Buyer nor compliance with the terms of this agreement will:

28.1.1. cause the Company or any of the Subsidiaries to lose the benefit of any right or privilege it presently enjoys, or

28.1.2. relieve any person of any obligation to the Company or any of the Subsidiaries (whether contractual or otherwise), or enable any person to determine any such obligation or any right or benefit enjoyed by the Company or any of the Subsidiaries, or to exercise any right in respect of the Company or any of the Subsidiaries, or

28.1.3. give rise to, or cause to become exercisable, any right of pre-emption over the Sale Shares, or

28.1.4. entitle any person to receive from the Company or any of the Subsidiaries any finder's fee, brokerage or other commission in connection with the purchase of the Sale Shares by the Buyer, or

28.1.5. result in any customer or supplier being entitled to cease dealing with the Company or any of the Subsidiaries or to reduce substantially its existing level of business or to change the terms on which it deals with the Company or any of the Subsidiaries, or

28.1.6. so far as the Sellers are aware, result in any officer or senior Employee leaving the Company or any of the Subsidiaries, or

28.1.7. result in a breach of contract, law, regulation, order, judgment, injunction, undertaking, decree or other like imposition, or

28.1.8. result in the loss or impairment of or any default under any licence, authorisation or consent required by the Company or any of the Subsidiaries for the purposes of its business, or

28.1.9. result in the creation, imposition, crystallisation or enforcement of any Encumbrance on any of the assets of the Company or the Subsidiaries, or

28.1.10. result in any present or future indebtedness of the Company or any of the Subsidiaries becoming due and payable, or capable of being declared due and payable, prior to its stated maturity date or in any financial facility of the Company or any of the Subsidiaries being withdrawn, or

28.1.11. entitle any person to acquire, or affect the entitlement of any person to acquire, shares in the Company.

29. RETIREMENT BENEFITS

29.1. The Pension Scheme[s] [is OR are] the only arrangement[s] under which the Company or any of the Subsidiaries has or may have any obligation (whether or not legally binding) to provide or contribute towards pension, lump-sum, death, ill-health, disability or accident benefits in respect of its past or present officers and employees (Pensionable Employees). No proposal or announcement has been made to any Employee or officer of the Company or any of the Subsidiaries as to the introduction, continuance, increase or improvement of, or the payment of a contribution towards, any other pension, lump-sum, death, ill-health, disability or accident benefit.

29.2. Full details of the Pension Scheme[s] are set out in the Disclosure Letter, including (but not limited to):

29.2.1. copies of all documents governing the Pension Scheme[s] and of any announcements and explanatory booklets relating to it,

29.2.2. the two latest annual reports and accounts of the Pension Scheme[s],

29.2.3. a list of all Pensionable Employees who are members of the Pension Scheme[s] with all details relevant to their membership and necessary to establish their entitlements under the Pension Scheme[s],

29.2.4. for each Pension Scheme that provides defined benefits, a true and complete copy of the most recent actuarial valuation of the Pension Scheme and a true and complete copy of all subsequent actuarial advice,

29.2.5. for each Pension Scheme that is an occupational pension scheme, all reports relating to the investment of the assets of the Pension Scheme during the last year and a list showing each asset of the Pension Scheme and its market value as at a date no earlier than one month before the date of this agreement, and

29.2.6. all agreements for the provision of services and any insurance contracts relating to the Pension Scheme[s].

The documents listed above contain full details of all benefits payable in respect of the Pensionable Employees under the Pension Scheme[s] (including any benefits payable to any Pensionable Employee on early retirement or redundancy under the Pension Scheme[s], or any previous scheme of which the Pensionable Employee was a member). No power to increase those benefits or to provide different benefits has been exercised, and there are no circumstances in which there is a practice of exercising such a power under the Pension Scheme[s].

29.3. All contributions, insurance premiums, tax and expenses due to and in respect of the Pension Scheme[s] have been duly paid. There are no liabilities outstanding in respect of the Pension Scheme[s] at the date of this agreement. The contributions in respect of the Pension Scheme[s] have been paid at the rates set out in the most recent schedule of contributions or the most recent payment schedule.

29.4. All death and disability benefits provided to the employees of the Company and Subsidiaries are fully insured by an insurance policy with an insurer of good repute. The Company and the Subsidiaries are not aware of any reason why these policies might be invalidated, or why the insurer might try to set them aside.

29.5. The Disclosure Letter has details of the rates at which the Company's, any Subsidiaries' and employees' contributions to the Pension Scheme[s] are being paid and how they are calculated, and whether they are paid in advance or in arrears. All amounts due to the Pension Scheme[s] have been paid.

29.6. No contribution notice or financial support direction under the Pensions Act 2004 has been issued to the Company or to any Subsidiary or to any other person in respect of any Pension Scheme and there is no fact or circumstance likely to give rise to any such notice or direction.

29.7. Each Pension Scheme is a registered pension scheme for the purposes of Chapter 2 of Part 4 of the Finance Act 2004 and there is no reason why HM Revenue & Customs might de-register the scheme.

29.8. If the Pension Scheme is a contracted-out scheme within the meaning of the Pension Schemes Act 1993, there is in force a contracting-out certificate covering the Company and the Subsidiaries and there is no reason why the certificate might be cancelled. No Pension Scheme that provides money purchase benefits is contracted out on a final salary basis.

29.9. Each Pension Scheme has been designed to comply with, and has been administered in accordance with, all applicable legal and administrative requirements and in compliance with its governing documents. The Company, the Subsidiaries [and, in the case of any Pension Scheme that is an occupational pension scheme, the trustees of that scheme] have complied in all material respects with their obligations under and in respect of the Pension Scheme[s].

29.10. For any Pension Scheme that provides defined benefits, the Actuary's report on the latest actuarial valuation describes the financial position of that scheme at its effective date. Nothing has happened since that date which would affect the level of funding of that Pension Scheme to a material extent. Since that date, contributions have been paid to that scheme at the rate[s] recommended by the Actuary. No assets have been withdrawn from that Pension Scheme (except to pay benefits) since the effective date of the list of assets disclosed in the Disclosure Letter.

29.11. [The Company and the Subsidiaries have provided access to a designated stakeholder scheme for their Pensionable Employees who are not members of the Pension Scheme, as required by section 3 of the Welfare Reform and Pensions Act 1999 OR The Company and the Subsidiaries are exempt from providing access to a stakeholder scheme for their Pensionable Employees.]

29.12. Neither the Company nor the Subsidiaries [nor the trustees of any Pension Scheme that is an occupational pension scheme] have discriminated against, or in relation to, any Pensionable Employee on grounds of age, sex, disability, marital status, hours of work, fixed-term or temporary agency worker status, sexual orientation, religion or belief in providing pension, lump-sum, death, ill-health, disability or accident benefits.

29.13. No claims or complaints have been made or are pending or threatened in relation to the Pension Scheme[s] or otherwise in respect of the provision of (or failure to provide) pension, lump-sum, death, ill-health, disability or accident benefits by the Company or any of the Subsidiaries in relation to any of the Pensionable Employees. There are no facts or circumstances likely to give rise to such claims or complaints.

29.14. No acts, omissions or other events have been reported to the Pensions Regulator under sections 69 or 70 of the Pensions Act 2004 and there is no fact or circumstance likely to give rise to such reports.

29.15. The Pension Scheme[s] do[es] not and [has OR have] not accepted any contributions from a European employer as defined for the purposes of Part 7 of the Pensions Act 2004.

29.16. For any Pension Scheme that provides defined benefits, there has been no arrangement which might be construed as a compromise or a reduction of a statutory debt under section 75 or 75A of the Pensions Act 1995.

29.17. For any Pension Scheme that provides defined benefits, there is no amount that is treated as a debt due to the trustees of that Pension Scheme, or from the Company or any Subsidiary to the trustees of any other pension scheme, under section 75 or 75A of the Pensions Act 1995 (or its predecessor, section 144 of the Pension Schemes Act 1993). Neither the Company nor any Subsidiary has ever participated in any occupational pension scheme other than the Pension Scheme[s].

29.18. If any Pension Scheme is a money purchase scheme, that scheme provides money purchase benefits only as defined in section 181 of the Pension Schemes Act 1993.

Part 2 - Tax warranties

1   GENERAL

1.1   All notices, returns (including any land transaction returns), reports, accounts, computations, statements, assessments and registrations and any other necessary information submitted by the Company or any Subsidiary to any

Taxation Authority for the purposes of Taxation have been made on a proper basis, were submitted within applicable time limits, were accurate and complete when submitted and remain accurate and complete in all material respects. None of the above is, or is likely to be, the subject of any material dispute with any Taxation Authority.

1.2 All Taxation (whether of the UK or elsewhere), for which the Company or any Subsidiary has been liable to account, has been duly paid (insofar as such Taxation ought to have been paid).

1.3 The Company and each Subsidiary have, within applicable time limits, kept and maintained complete and accurate records, invoices and other information in relation to Taxation as they are required or is prudent to keep and maintain. Such records, invoices and information form part of tax accounting arrangements that enable the tax liabilities of the Company and any Subsidiary to be calculated accurately in all material respects.

1.4 The Company and each Subsidiary have complied within applicable time limits with all notices served on them and any other requirements lawfully made of them by any Taxation Authority.

1.5 [Neither the Company nor any Subsidiary has made any payments representing instalments of corporation tax pursuant to the Corporation Tax (Instalment Payments) Regulations 1998 in respect of any current or preceding accounting periods nor is under any obligation to do so.]

OR

[The Company is not OR The Disclosure Letter discloses whether or not the Company or any Subsidiary] is a large company within the meaning of regulation 3 of the Corporation Tax (Instalment Payment) Regulations 1998.]

1.6 Neither the Company nor any Subsidiary has received from any Taxation Authority (and has not subsequently repaid to or settled with that Taxation Authority) any payment to which it was not entitled, or any notice in which its liability to Taxation was understated.

1.7 Neither the Company nor any Subsidiary has paid, within the period of [seven] years ending on the date of this agreement, or will become liable to pay any penalty, fine, surcharge or interest charged by virtue of the TMA 1970 or any other Taxation Statute.

1.8 All Taxation and national insurance contributions deductible and payable under the PAYE system and/or any other Taxation Statute has, so far as is required to be deducted, been deducted from all payments made (or treated as made) by the Company or any Subsidiary. All amounts due to be paid to the relevant Taxation Authority prior to the date of this agreement have been so paid by the due date, including, without limitation, all Tax chargeable on benefits provided for directors, employees or former employees of the Company or any Subsidiary or any persons required to be treated as such.

1.9 Proper records have been maintained in respect of all such deductions and payments, and all applicable regulations have been complied with.

1.10 The Disclosure Letter contains details (so far as they affect the Company or any Subsidiary) of all current dispensations agreed with HM Revenue & Customs in relation to PAYE and all notifications given by HM Revenue & Customs under section 65(6) of ITEPA 2003.

1.11 Neither the Company nor any Subsidiary is involved in any dispute with any Taxation Authority nor has, within the past [12 months], been subject to any visit, audit, investigation, discovery or access order by any Taxation Authority. The Seller is not aware of any circumstances existing which make it likely that a visit, audit, investigation, discovery or access order will be made in the next [12 months].

1.12 [The amount of Taxation chargeable on the Company or any Subsidiary during any accounting period ending on or within the six years before Completion has not, to any material extent, depended on any concession, agreement or other formal or informal arrangement with any Taxation Authority.

OR

Neither the Company nor any Subsidiary has, for any period after the Accounts Date, taken any action which has had or might have the result of altering, prejudicing or in any way disturbing for any period commencing after the Accounts Date any concession, agreement or other formal or informal arrangement which it has previously negotiated with any Taxation Authority and the Disclosure Letter contains details of such concessions, agreements or arrangements.]

1.13 All transactions in respect of which any clearance or consent was required from any Taxation Authority have been entered into by the Company or any Subsidiary after such consent or clearance has been properly obtained. Any application for such clearance or consent has been made on the basis of full and accurate disclosure of all the relevant material facts and considerations, and all such transactions have been carried into effect only in accordance with the terms of the relevant clearance or consent.

1.14 The Company and the Subsidiaries have duly submitted all claims, disclaimers and elections the making of which has been assumed for the purposes of the Accounts. No such claims, disclaimers or elections are likely to be disputed or withdrawn.

1.15 The Disclosure Letter contains full particulars of all matters relating to Taxation in respect of which the Company or any Subsidiary is, or at Completion, will be entitled to:

1.15.1 make any claim (including a supplementary claim), disclaimer or election for relief under any Taxation Statute or other provision, and/or

1.15.2 appeal against any assessment or determination relating to Taxation, and/or

1.15.3 apply for a postponement of Taxation.

1.16 Neither the Company nor any Subsidiary is, or will become liable, to make to any person (including any Taxation Authority) any payment in respect of any liability to Taxation which is primarily or directly chargeable against, or attributable to, any other person (other than the Company or any Subsidiary).

1.17 The Accounts make full provision or reserve within generally accepted accounting principles for any period ending on or before the date to which they were drawn up for all Taxation assessed or liable to be assessed on the Company or the relevant Subsidiary, or for which the Company or the relevant Subsidiary is accountable at that date, whether or not the Company or that Subsidiary has (or may have) the right of reimbursement against any other person. Proper provision has been made and shown in the Accounts for deferred taxation in accordance with generally accepted accounting principles.

1.18 The Company and each Subsidiary has sufficient records to determine the tax consequence which would arise on any disposal or realisation of any asset owned at the Accounts Date or acquired since that date, but prior to Completion.

1.19 Neither the Company nor any Subsidiary has entered into a Managed Payment Plan within the provisions of section 111 of the Finance Act 2009 (paragraph 80 of Schedule 7 to the Taxation (International and Other Provisions) Act 2010) nor into any arrangement with HM Revenue & Customs for the deferred payment of any liability to Taxation.

1.20 Neither the Company nor any Subsidiary is a qualifying company within the meaning of Schedule 46 to the Finance Act 2009.

2 CHARGEABLE GAINS

2.1 The book value shown in, or adopted for the purposes, of the Accounts as the value of each of the assets of the Company or any Subsidiary, on the disposal of which a chargeable gain or allowable loss could arise, does not exceed the amount which on a disposal of such asset at the date of this agreement would be deductible, in each case, disregarding any statutory right to claim any allowance or relief other than amounts deductible under section 38 of TCGA 1992.

2.2 There has been no transaction to which any of the following provisions applies, or could apply, in respect of any asset held by the Company or any Subsidiary:

2.2.1 section 23 of TCGA 1992 (compensation and insurance monies),

2.2.2 section 135 and 136 of TCGA 1992 (reconstructions and amalgamations),

2.2.3 section 139 of TCGA 1992 (transfers of assets on reconstructions and amalgamations),

2.2.4 section 152-154 (inclusive) of TCGA 1992 (replacement of business assets),

2.2.5 sections 140A and 140C of TCGA 1992 (transfer of a trade),

2.2.6 section 165 of TCGA 1992 (gifts of business assets),

2.2.7 section 171-173 (inclusive) of TCGA 1992 (intra-group transfers),

2.2.8 section 247-248 of TCGA 1992 (compulsory acquisitions), and

2.2.9 section 242(2) of TCGA 1992 (small part disposals of land).

2.3 Neither the Company nor any Subsidiary has been a party to any scheme or arrangement whereby the value of an asset has been materially reduced as set out in sections 29-34 of TCGA 1992.

2.4 Neither the Company nor any Subsidiary has made any election under section 35(5) of TCGA 1992 and the Accounts have not been prepared on the basis that such an election will be made.

2.5 Neither the Company nor any Subsidiary owns, or has owned, any asset on the disposal of which paragraph 2 of Schedule 3 to TCGA 1992 would apply.

2.6 Neither the Company nor any Subsidiary holds any asset on the disposal of which Schedule 4 to TCGA 1992 may apply.

2.7 Neither the Company nor any Subsidiary has transferred a trade carried on by it outside the UK in circumstances such that a chargeable gain may be deemed to arise at a date after such transfer under section 140 of TCGA 1992.

2.8 Neither the Company nor any Subsidiary owns any assets which are wasting assets within the meaning of section 44 of TCGA 1992 and which do not qualify in full for an allowance under the provisions of CAA 2001.

2.9 Neither the Company nor any Subsidiary has disposed of or acquired any asset in circumstances falling within section 17 or 19 of TCGA 1992.

2.10 Neither the Company nor any Subsidiary is owed a debt on a security, the disposal or satisfaction of which will give rise to a liability to corporation tax on chargeable gains by reason of section 251 of TCGA 1992.

2.11 Neither the Company nor any Subsidiary has received any assets by way of gift as mentioned in section 282 of TCGA 1992 and neither the Company nor any Subsidiary has held, or holds, shares in a company to which section 125 of TCGA 1992 could apply.

2.12 No claim or election affecting the Company or any Subsidiary has been made (or assumed to be made) under section 187 of TCGA 1992.

2.13 Neither the Company nor any Subsidiary has made a part disposal of any assets for the purposes of section 42 of TCGA 1992.

2.14 Neither the Company nor any Subsidiary has, since the Accounts Date, appropriated any of its assets to or from trading stock for the purposes of section 161 of TCGA 1992.

2.15 Neither the Company nor any Subsidiary is, or may become, liable to tax under section 190 of TCGA 1992 in respect of a disposal occurring on or before Completion.

2.16 No assessment in respect of a capital gain on the disposal of any asset situated outside the UK or of unremittable overseas income has been postponed under section 279 of TCGA 1992 or section 584 of ICTA 1988 (replaced with effect from 1 April 2009, for accounting periods ending on or after that date, by section 1275 of the Corporation Tax Act 2009) in relation to the Company or any Subsidiary.

2.17 Neither the Company nor any Subsidiary has acquired shares on a reorganisation (within the meaning of section 126 of TCGA 1992) in circumstances such that part of the consideration given by the Company or any Subsidiary would be disallowed under section 128(2) of that Act.

3   CAPITAL LOSSES

3.1   No capital loss has accrued to the Company or any Subsidiary that is a loss within the meaning of either section 8 or section 16A of TCGA 1992.

3.2   No allowable loss has accrued to the Company or any Subsidiary to which section 18(3) of TCGA 1992 would apply.

3.3   No loss which might accrue on the disposal by the Company or any Subsidiary of any asset is liable to be reduced or eliminated by the application of section 35(3) or (4) of TCGA 1992.

3.4   No allowable loss which might accrue on the disposal by the Company or any Subsidiary of any share in, or security of, any company is likely to be reduced by virtue of sections 176 and 177 of TCGA 1992.

3.5   Neither the Company nor any Subsidiary has any pre-entry loss, as defined in paragraph 1(2)(a) or (b) of Schedule 7A to TCGA 1992, and there is no allowable loss accrued, or which might accrue, on the disposal of any asset of the Company or any Subsidiary which could be treated as a pre-entry loss as so defined following Completion.

3.6   The Disclosure Letter gives details of any loss accruing to the Company or any Subsidiary in respect of which notice needs to be, but has not been,given to an officer of HM Revenue & Customs in order to be an allowable loss for the purposes of TCGA 1992.

4   CAPITAL ALLOWANCES

4.1   If any asset of the Company or any Subsidiary were disposed of at Completion for its book value as shown in, or adopted for the purpose of, the Accounts, or for the value of consideration actually given for it on its acquisition (if such asset were acquired since the Accounts Date), no balancing charge under CAA 2001 (or any other legislation relating to capital allowances) or similar clawback of relief in jurisdictions outside the UK would be made on the Company or that Subsidiary.

4.2   No event has occurred since the Accounts Date (otherwise than in the ordinary course of business) whereby any balancing charge may fall to be made against, or any disposal value may fall to be brought into account by, the Company or any Subsidiary under CAA 2001 (or any other legislation relating to any capital allowances) or similar legislation relating to relief for similar capital expenditure in jurisdictions outside of the UK.

4.3   All expenditure which the Company and Subsidiaries have incurred (or may incur) under any subsisting commitment for the provision of plant or machinery has qualified, or will qualify (if not deductible as a trading expense of the Company or Subsidiary), for allowances at the applicable rate under CAA 2001. The Company has notified its Inspector of Taxes of all such expenditure.

4.4   Neither the Company nor any Subsidiary has made any claim for capital allowances in respect of any asset which is leased to or from, or hired to or from, the Company or any Subsidiary. No election affecting the Company or any Subsidiary has been made, or agreed to be made, under sections 177 or 183 of CAA 2001 in respect of such assets.

4.5   Neither the Company nor any Subsidiary is a lessee under a lease to which Chapter 17 of Part 2 of CAA 2001 apply or could apply.

4.6   Neither the Company nor any Subsidiary is a party to any transactions to which Schedule 12 to the Finance Act 1997 apply or could apply.

4.7   Neither the Company nor any Subsidiary has made any election under section 83 of CAA 2001, nor is it taken to have made such an election under section 89(4) of CAA 2001.

4.8   Neither the Company nor any Subsidiary has incurred any long-life asset expenditure within the meaning of section 90 of CAA 2001.

4.9   None of the assets of the Company or any Subsidiary, expenditure on which has qualified for a capital allowance under Part 3 of CAA 2001, has at any time been used otherwise than as an industrial building or structure.

4.10   The Disclosure Letter gives full details of any disclaimers of allowances on plant and machinery and of any reduction in initial allowances on industrial and agricultural buildings.

4.11   Neither the Company nor any Subsidiary has claimed any research and development tax relief or tax credit nor any first-year tax credits (within the meaning of section 262A of, and Schedule 1A to, CAA 2001)

4.12   The Disclosure Letter gives full details of the residue of qualifying expenditure for all assets of the Company or any Subsidiary which are industrial buildings for the purposes of Part 3 of CAA 2001.

4.13   Neither the company nor any Subsidiary has incurred any expenditure which qualifies for allowances under Part 3A of CAA 2001 (business premises renovation allowance).

4.14   The Disclosure Letter gives full details of all expenditure incurred on the provision of or replacement of integral features (within the meaning of section 33A of CAA 2001).

5   **DISTRIBUTIONS AND OTHER PAYMENTS**

5.1   No distribution or deemed distribution, within the meaning of sections 209, 210 or 211 of ICTA 1988 (section 1000 of the Corporation Tax Act 2010), has been made (or will be deemed to have been made) by the Company or any Subsidiary, except dividends shown in their audited accounts, and neither the Company nor any Subsidiary is bound to make any such distribution.

5.2   No rents, interest, annual payments or other sums of an income nature, paid or payable by the Company or any Subsidiary, or which the Company or any Subsidiary is under an existing obligation to pay in the future, are or may be wholly or partially disallowable as deductions, management expenses or charges in computing taxable profits for Taxation purposes.

5.3   Neither the Company nor any Subsidiary has, within the period of seven years preceding Completion, been engaged in, nor been a party to, any of the transactions set out in sections 213 to 218 (inclusive) of ICTA 1988 (Chapter 5 of Part 23 of the Corporation Tax Act 2010), nor has it made or received a chargeable payment as defined in section 214 of ICTA 1988 (section 1086 of the Corporation Tax Act 2010).

5.4   Neither the Company nor any Subsidiary has received, or is likely to receive, a dividend which is not exempt within the provisions set out in chapters 2 and 3 of Part 9A of the Corporation Tax Act 2009.

5.5   Neither the Company nor any Subsidiary has received any capital distribution to which section 189 of TCGA 1992 could apply.

6   LOAN RELATIONSHIPS

6.1   All interests, discounts and premiums payable by the Company or any Subsidiary in respect of its loan relationships (within the meaning of section 302 of the Corporation Tax Act 2009, formerly section 81 of the Finance Act 1996) are eligible to be brought into account by the Company or the Subsidiaries as a debit for the purposes of Part 5 of the Corporation Tax Act 2009 (formerly Chapter II of Part IV of the Finance Act 1996) at the time, and to the extent that such debits are recognised in the statutory accounts of the Company or the Subsidiaries.

6.2   Neither the Company nor any Subsidiary is, or in the six years prior to Completion has been, party to a debtor relationship (within the meaning of section 302(6) of the Corporation Tax Act 2009, formerly section 103 of the Finance Act 1996) to which Chapter 8 of Part 5 of the Corporation Tax Act 2009 (formerly paragraph 2 of Schedule 9 to the Finance Act 1996) applies or may apply.

6.3   Neither the Company nor any Subsidiary is party to a loan relationship made other than on arm's length terms. There are no circumstances in which section 445 or 447 of the Corporation Tax Act 2009 (formerly paragraphs 11 and 11A of Schedule 9 to the Finance Act 1996) could apply to require an adjustment of debits and/or credits brought into account by the Company or any Subsidiary.

6.4   The Disclosure Letter contains full particulars of any debtor relationship (within the meaning of section 302(6) of the Corporation Tax Act 2009, formerly section 103 of the Finance Act 1996) of the Company and the Subsidiaries which relates to any deeply discounted security (within the meaning of Chapter 8 of Part 4 of the Income Tax (Trading and Other Income Act) 2005) to which sections 406-412 of the Corporation Tax Act 2009 (formerly paragraphs 17 or 18 of Schedule 9 to the Finance Act 1996) apply.

6.5   Neither the Company nor any Subsidiary has been a party to a loan relationship which had an unallowable purpose (within the meaning of section 442 of the Corporation Tax Act 2009, formerly paragraph 13 of Schedule 9 to the Finance Act 1996).

7   CLOSE COMPANIES

[Neither the Company nor any Subsidiary is, nor has ever been, a close company within the meaning of sections 414 and 415 of ICTA 1988 (section 439 of the Corporation Tax Act 2010).

OR

7.1   Neither the Company nor any Subsidiary is, or has ever been, a close investment-holding company as defined in section 13A of ICTA 1988 (section 34 of the Corporation Tax Act 2010).

7.2   No distribution within section 418 of ICTA 1988 (section 1064 of the Corporation Tax Act 2010) has been made by the Company or any Subsidiary during the last six years ending at the Accounts Date, nor have such distributions been made between the Accounts Date and Completion.

7.3   Any loans or advances made, or agreed to be made, by the Company or any Subsidiary within sections 419 or 422 of ICTA 1988 (sections 455, 459 and 460 of the Corporation Tax Act 2010) have been disclosed in the Disclosure Letter. Neither the Company nor any Subsidiary has released or written off, or agreed to release or write off, the whole or any part of any such loans or advances.]

8   GROUP RELIEF

8.1   The Disclosure Letter contains full particulars of every written agreement relating to the claim or surrender of group relief (as defined by section 402 of ICTA 1988 (section 99 of the Corporation Tax Act 2010)) to which the Company or any Subsidiary is, or has been, a party within the last seven years.

8.2   All claims made by the Company and the Subsidiaries for group relief were valid when made and have been or will be allowed by way of relief from corporation tax. The Company and the Subsidiaries have met all procedural and other requirements of Part VIII of Schedule 18 to the Finance Act 1998 in respect of such claims.

8.3   Except as provided in the Accounts, neither the Company nor any Subsidiary is, or will be, obliged to make or be entitled to receive any payment for group relief as defined in section 402(6) of ICTA 1988 (section 183 of the Corporation Tax Act 2010) in respect of any period ending on or before the Accounts Date.

8.4   Neither the Company nor any Subsidiary has been party to a surrender of a tax refund under section 102 of the Finance Act 1989 (section 963 of the Corporation Tax Act 2010).

9   GROUPS OF COMPANIES

9.1   The Company and any Subsidiary together comprise a group for the purposes of Part 5 of the Corporation Tax Act 2010 and, so far as the Seller is aware, there are no circumstances or arrangements as a result of which any Subsidiary or the Company will cease to form part of such group.

9.2   Neither the Company nor any Subsidiary has entered into, or agreed to enter into, an election pursuant to section 171A or section 179A of TCGA 1992 or pursuant to section 792 of the Corporation Tax Act 2009 (formerly paragraph 66 of Schedule 29 to the Finance Act 2002).

9.3   Neither the execution nor completion of this agreement, nor any other event since the Accounts Date, will result in any chargeable asset being deemed to have been disposed of and re-acquired by the Company or any Subsidiary for Taxation purposes under;

9.3.1   section 179 of TCGA 1992,

9.3.2   sections 345 and 346 of the Corporation Tax Act 2009 (formerly paragraph 12A of Schedule 9 to the Finance Act 1996),

9.3.3   sections 630-632 of the Corporation Tax Act 2009 (formerly paragraph 30A of Schedule 26 to the Finance Act 2002),

9.3.4   section 780 or 785 of the Corporation Tax Act 2009 (formerly paragraph 58 or 60 of Schedule 29 to the Finance Act 2002), or

9.3.5   as a result of any other Event (as defined in the Tax Covenant) since the Accounts Date.

9.4   Neither the Company nor any Subsidiary has made any election under section 179A of TCGA 1992 or section 792 of the Corporation Tax Act 2009 (formerly paragraph 66 of Schedule 29 to the Finance Act 2002).

9.5   Neither the Company nor any Subsidiary has any unrelieved surplus advance corporation tax eligible for carrying forward or has, in the seven years ending at Completion, set surplus advance corporation tax against corporation tax which could be displaced so as to give rise to a liability of the Company or any Subsidiary to make a payment of, or in respect of, corporation tax.

9.6   No change of ownership of the Company or any Subsidiary has taken place in circumstances such that sections 768 or 768A-E (inclusive) of ICTA 1988 (Part 14 of the Corporation Tax Act 2010) or Regulation 13(6) of the Corporation Tax (Treatment of Unrelieved Surplus Advance Corporation Tax) Regulations 1999 have, or may, be applied to deny relief for a loss or losses incurred by the Company or any Subsidiary. Within the period of three years ending with the date of this agreement, there has been no cessation of, or major change in the nature or conduct of, any trade or business (as defined for these purposes in section 768 of ICTA 1988 (section 673 of the Corporation Tax Act 2010)) carried on by the Company or any Subsidiary.

9.7   Neither the Company nor any Subsidiary has ever been party to any arrangements pursuant to section 36 of the Finance Act 1998 (paragraph 79 of Schedule 7 to the Taxation (International and Other Provisions) Act 2010) (group payment arrangements).

10   INTANGIBLE ASSETS

For the purposes of this paragraph 10, references to intangible fixed assets mean intangible fixed assets and goodwill within the meaning of Part 8 of the Corporation Tax Act 2009 (formerly Schedule 29 to the Finance Act 2002) and to which that legislation applies. References to an intangible fixed asset shall be construed accordingly.

10.1   The Disclosure Letter sets out the amount of expenditure on each of the intangible fixed assets of the Company and the Subsidiaries and provides the basis on which any debit relating to that expenditure has been taken into account in the Accounts or, in relation to expenditure incurred since the Accounts Date, will be available to the Company or any Subsidiary. No circumstances have arisen since the Accounts Date by reason of which that basis might change.

10.2   No claims or elections have been made by the Company or any Subsidiary under Chapter 7 of Part 8 of the Corporation Tax Act 2009 (formerly Part 7 of Schedule 29 to the Finance Act 2002), or section 827 of the Corporation Tax Act 2009 (formerly paragraph 86 of Schedule 29 to the Finance Act 2002) in respect of any intangible fixed asset of the Company or any Subsidiary.

10.3   Since the Accounts Date:

    10.3.1   neither the Company nor any Subsidiary owns an asset which has ceased to be a chargeable intangible asset in the circumstances described in section 859 of the Corporation Tax Act 2009 (formerly paragraph 108 of Schedule 29 to the Finance Act 2002),

    10.3.2   neither the Company nor any Subsidiary has realised or acquired an intangible fixed asset for the purposes of Part 8 of the Corporation Tax Act 2009 (formerly Schedule 29 to the Finance Act 2002), and

    10.3.3   no circumstances have arisen which have required, or will require, a credit to be brought into account by the Company or any Subsidiary on a revaluation of an intangible fixed asset.

11   COMPANY RESIDENCE, TREASURY CONSENTS AND OVERSEAS INTERESTS

11.1   The Company and the Subsidiaries have, throughout the past seven years, been resident in the UK for corporation tax purposes and have not, at any time in the past seven years, been treated as resident in any other jurisdiction for the purposes of any double taxation arrangements having effect under section 18 of the Corporation Tax Act 2009 (formerly section 249 of the Finance Act 1994) and section 788 of ICTA 1988 (section 2 of the Taxation (International and Other Provisions) Act 2010) or for any other tax purpose.

11.2   Neither the Company nor any Subsidiary has caused, permitted or entered into any of the transactions specified in section 765 of ICTA 1988 (migration of companies) or, in relation to transactions occurring on or after 1 July 2009, as set out in section 37 of and Schedule 17 to the Finance Act 2009 without the prior written consent of HM Treasury, or without having duly provided the required information to HM Revenue & Customs (as appropriate).

11.3   Neither the Company nor any Subsidiary would be a person to whom section 132(3) of the Finance Act 1988 (paragraph 54 Of Schedule 7 to the Taxation (International and Other Provisions) Act 2010) applies in relation to a migrating company.

11.4   Neither the Company nor any Subsidiary holds shares in a company which is not resident in the UK and which would be a close company if it were resident in the UK in circumstances such that a chargeable gain accruing to the company not resident in the UK could be apportioned to the Company and/or any Subsidiary pursuant to section 13 of TCGA 1992.

11.5   Neither the Company nor any Subsidiary is, or may become, liable to tax under Schedule 28 to the Finance Act 2000 (Chapter 7 of Part 22 of the Corporation Tax Act 2010) in respect of any amount of unpaid corporation tax of a non-UK resident company

11.6   Neither the Company nor any Subsidiary is holding, or has held in the past seven years, any interest in a controlled foreign company within section 747 of ICTA 1988. Neither the Company nor any Subsidiary has any material interest in an offshore fund as defined in section 759 of ICTA 1988 or in Part 1 of Schedule 22 to the Finance Act 2009.

11.7 Neither the Company nor any Subsidiary has received any foreign loan interest in respect of which double taxation relief will, or may, be restricted under section 798 of ICTA 1988.

11.8 No claim has been made by the Company or any Subsidiary under sections 584 or 585 of ICTA 1988 or section 1275 of the Corporation Tax Act 2009.

11.9 Neither the Company nor any Subsidiary has been a party to any transaction or arrangement whereby it is, or may become, liable for Taxation by virtue of sections 971 and 972 of the Income Tax Act 2007 (ITA 2007) (or regulations made under them) or section 126 of the Finance Act 1995.

11.10 Neither the Company nor any Subsidiary has, or within the last seven years has had, a permanent establishment outside the UK.

11.11 Neither the Company nor any Subsidiary is an agent or permanent establishment of another company, person, business or enterprise for the purpose of assessing such company, person, business or enterprise to Taxation in the country of residence of the Company or any Subsidiary.

11.12 Neither the Company nor any Subsidiary is, or has been within the past seven years, a dual residence company for the purposes of section 404 of ICTA 1988 (section 109 of the Corporation Tax Act 2010).

12   TRANSFER PRICING

12.1 All transactions or arrangements made by the Company or any Subsidiary have been made on fully arm's length terms. There are no circumstances in which section 770A of, or Schedule 28AA to, ICTA 1988 (Part 4 of the Taxation (International and Other Provisions) Act 2010) or any other rule or provision could apply causing any Taxation Authority to make an adjustment to the terms on which such transaction or arrangement is treated as being made for Taxation purposes.

12.2 In relation to each transaction for the supply of goods or services or the lending or borrowing of money into which the Company or any Subsidiary has entered with a party with which it was connected, the Company or the relevant Subsidiary has full contemporaneous documentary evidence of the process used to establish that arm's length terms applied.

13   ANTI-AVOIDANCE

13.1 Neither the Company nor any Subsidiary has been a party to, nor has been otherwise involved in, any transaction, scheme or arrangement designed wholly or mainly or containing steps or stages having no commercial purpose and designed wholly or mainly for the purpose of avoiding or deferring Taxation or reducing a liability to Taxation or amounts to be accounted for under PAYE.

13.2 Neither the Company nor any Subsidiary has, at any time, been a party to or otherwise involved in a transaction or series of transactions in relation to which advisers considered that there was a risk that the Company or any Subsidiary could be liable to Taxation as a result of the principles in W. T. Ramsey Limited v IRC (54 TC 101) or Furniss v Dawson (55 TC 324), as developed in subsequent cases, or as a result of the principles in Halifax (C-255/02) as developed in subsequent cases.

13.3   Neither the Company nor any Subsidiary has entered into any notifiable arrangements for the purposes of Part 7 of the Finance Act 2004 any notifiable contribution arrangement for the purpose of the National Insurance Contribution (Application of Part 7 of the Finance Act 2004) Regulations 2007 (SI 2007/785) or any notifiable schemes for the purposes of Schedule 11A to the VATA 1994.

14   INHERITANCE TAX

14.1   Neither the Company nor any Subsidiary has:

14.1.1   made any transfer of value within sections 94 and 202 of IHTA 1984, or

14.1.2   received any value such that liability might arise under section 199 of IHTA 1984, or

14.1.3   been a party to associated operations in relation to a transfer of value as defined by section 268 of IHTA 1984.

14.2   There is no unsatisfied liability to inheritance tax attached to, or attributable to, the Sale Shares or any asset of the Company or any Subsidiary. None of them are subject to any Inland Revenue charge as mentioned in section 237 and 238 of IHTA 1984.

14.3   No asset owned by the Company or any Subsidiary, nor the Sale Shares, are liable to be subject to any sale, mortgage or charge by virtue of section 212(1) of IHTA 1984.

15   VALUE ADDED TAX

15.1   [The Company and the Subsidiaries are each taxable persons and are duly registered for the purposes of VAT.

OR

The Company and the Subsidiaries are members of a group for VAT purposes of which [NAME] is the representative member with quarterly prescribed accounting periods, such registration not being pursuant to paragraph 2 of Schedule 1 to VATA 1994 or subject to any conditions imposed by or agreed with HM Revenue & Customs. Neither the Company nor any Subsidiary is (nor are there any circumstances in which they may become) under a duty to make monthly payments on account under the Value Added Tax (Payments on Account) Order 1993.]

15.2   The Company and the Subsidiaries have each complied with all statutory provisions, rules, regulations, orders and directions in respect of VAT, promptly submitted accurate returns, and maintained full and accurate VAT records, invoices and other requisite documents. Neither the Company nor any Subsidiary has been:

15.2.1   subject to any interest, forfeiture, surcharge or penalty, or

15.2.2   given any notice under sections 59, 59A or 64 of VATA 1994, or

15.2.3   given a warning within section 76(2) of VATA 1994, or

15.2.4   required to give security under paragraph 4 of Schedule 11 to VATA 1994.

15.3   VAT has been duly paid by the Company and each Subsidiary, or provision has been made in the Accounts for all amounts of VAT for which the Company and each of the Subsidiaries is liable.

15.4   All supplies made by the Company or any Subsidiary are taxable supplies. Neither the Company nor any Subsidiary has been, or will be, denied full credit for all input tax under sections 25 and 26 of VATA 1994 (and regulations made under it) or for any other reasons. All VAT paid or payable by the Company or any Subsidiary is input tax as defined in section 24 of VATA 1994 and regulations made under it.

15.5   [Neither the Company nor any Subsidiary is, or has been, for VAT purposes, a member of any group of companies other than the group comprising the Company and the Subsidiaries alone. No act or transaction has been effected in consequence of which the Company or any Subsidiary, is or may be held, liable for any VAT arising from supplies made by another company. No direction has been given, nor will be given, by HM Revenue & Customs under Schedule 9A to VATA 1994 as a result of which the Company or any Subsidiary would be treated as a member of another group for the purposes of VAT.

OR

The Disclosure Letter contains full details of [each OR the] group registration, including details of each company which has, or has been, in the period of six years ending with the date of Completion, a member of that group.]

15.6   Neither the Company nor any Subsidiary has been, or agreed to be, a party to any transaction or arrangement in relation to which a direction has been, or could be, made under paragraph 1 of Schedule 6 or paragraph 1 of Schedule 7 to VATA 1994.

15.7   Neither the Company nor any Subsidiary is, or has agreed to become, liable for VAT under sections 47, 48 or 55 of VATA 1994. No direction has been given, or may be given, by HM Revenue & Customs under paragraph 2 of Schedule 6 to VATA 1994.

15.8   For the purposes of Schedule 10 to VATA 1994, the Company, any Subsidiary and any relevant associates of such companies (within the meaning of paragraph 3 of Schedule 10 to VATA 1994) have exercised an option to tax (pursuant to paragraph 2 of Schedule 10 to VATA 1994) only in respect of those Properties listed as having been the subject of such an option in the Disclosure Letter and:

15.8.1   neither the Company nor any Subsidiary or relevant associate of such companies has any intention of exercising, or obligation to exercise, such an option in respect of any other of the Properties,

15.8.2   all things necessary for the option to have effect have been done and, in particular, any notification and information required by paragraph 20 of Schedule 10 to VATA 1994 has been given and any permission required by paragraph 28 of Schedule 10 to VATA 1994 has been properly obtained,

15.8.3   a copy of the notification, and of any permission obtained from HM

Revenue & Customs in connection with the option, is included in the Disclosure Letter,

15.8.4 no option has or will be revoked or rendered ineffective under paragraph 12 of Schedule 10 to VATA 1994,

15.8.5 neither the Company nor any Subsidiary or relevant associate of such companies (within the meaning of paragraph 3 of Schedule 10 to VATA 1994) has charged VAT, whether on rents or otherwise, which is not properly chargeable, and

15.8.6 neither the Company nor any Subsidiary or relevant associate of such companies has agreed to refrain from exercising an option in relation to any of the Properties.

15.8.7 neither the Company nor any Subsidiary or relevant associate of such companies has made a real estate election within the meaning of paragraph 21 of Schedule 10 VATA 1994 in relation to any property.

15.9 Neither the Company nor any Subsidiary owns, or has at any time within the period of ten years preceding the date of this agreement owned, any assets which are capital items that are subject to the capital goods scheme under Part XV of the VAT Regulations 1995.

15.10 Neither the Company nor any Subsidiary has made any claim for bad debt relief under section 36 of VATA 1994. There are no existing circumstances by virtue of which any refund of VAT obtained or claimed may be required to be repaid.

15.11 Neither the Company nor any Subsidiary has entered into any self-billing arrangement (in the circumstances provided in section 29 of VATA 1994) in respect of supplies made by any other person, nor has it at any time agreed to allow any such person to make out VAT invoices in respect of supplies made by the Company or any Subsidiary.

15.12 The Disclosure Letter contains full particulars of all claims which have been, or could be, made by the Company or any Subsidiary under sections 78 or 79 of VATA 1994. There are no circumstances under which an assessment under section 78A of VATA 1994 has been, or could be, made on the Company or any Subsidiary.

15.13 In relation to the cross-border VAT changes which took effect from 1 January 2010 under the provisions of section 76 to 78 of and Schedule 36 to the Finance Act 2009:

15.13.1 the Company and each Subsidiary has a record of the VAT registration number of all EU business customers and has provided its own VAT registration number to all its suppliers who are resident in an EU Member State,

15.13.2 the accounting system of the Company and each Subsidiary requires no modifications in order to produce promptly and accurately the information required for completion of the EC sales lists,

15.13.3 neither the Company nor any Subsidiary supplies or purchases cross-border services the VAT treatment of which will be affected by the changes in the place or time of supply rules,

15.13.4 no repayments of VAT have been claimed by the Company or any Subsidiary in the 12 months ending on Completion from the tax authorities of any EU Member State other than the UK, and as at Completion, neither the Company nor any Subsidiary will have any outstanding entitlement to make such a claim.

16 PREMIUMS AND SALE AND LEASE BACK OF LAND

Neither the Company nor any Subsidiary has entered into any transaction to which Chapter 4 of Part 4 of the Corporation Tax Act 2009 (formerly sections 34, 35, 36 of ICTA 1988), 43A-G or 779-784 (inclusive) of ICTA 1988 (Part 19 of the Corporation Tax Act 2010) have been, or could be, applied.

17 EMPLOYEES AND PENSIONS

17.1 Neither the Company nor any Subsidiary has made, or agreed to make, any payment to, or provided or agreed to provide any benefit for, any director or former director, officer or employee of the Company or any Subsidiary, whether as compensation for loss of office, termination of employment or otherwise, which is not allowable as a deduction in calculating the profits of the Company or relevant Subsidiary for Taxation purposes, whether up to or after the Accounts Date.

17.2 Neither the Company nor any Subsidiary participates in a scheme under section 713 of ITEPA 2003.

17.3 The Disclosure Letter contains details of all schemes approved by HM Revenue & Customs under Schedules 2, 3 and 4 to Income Tax (Earnings and Pensions) Act 2003 (Approved Schemes) and of all options granted under Schedule 5 to Income Tax (Earnings and Pensions) Act 2003 (EMI Options). Neither the Company nor any Subsidiary is aware of any circumstances under which HM Revenue & Customs may withdraw approval of any Approved Scheme, or which might cause a disqualifying event under section 534 of ITEPA 2003 in respect of any EMI Options.

18 STAMP DUTY, STAMP DUTY LAND TAX AND STAMP DUTY RESERVE TAX

18.1 Any document that may be necessary or desirable in proving the title of the Company or any Subsidiary to any asset which is owned by the Company or any Subsidiary at Completion, and each document which the Company or any Subsidiary may wish to enforce or produce in evidence, is duly stamped for stamp duty purposes. No such documents which are outside the UK would attract stamp duty if they were brought into the UK.

18.2 Neither entering into this agreement nor Completion will result in the withdrawal of a stamp duty or stamp duty land tax relief granted on or before Completion which will affect the Company or any Subsidiary.

18.3 No circumstances exist under which paragraph 5 or paragraph 12 of Schedule 7 to the Finance Act 2003 (recovery of relief from another group company or controlling director) could apply to the Company or any Subsidiary.

18.4   The Disclosure Letter sets out full and accurate details of any chargeable interest (as defined under section 48 of the Finance Act 2003) acquired or held by the Company or any Subsidiary before Completion in respect of which the Sellers are aware, or ought reasonably to be aware, that an additional land transaction return will be required to be filed with a Taxation Authority and/or a payment of stamp duty land tax made on or after Completion.

18.5   Since the Accounts Date, neither the Company nor any Subsidiary has incurred any liability to, or been accountable for, any stamp duty reserve tax. There has been no agreement within section 87(1) of the Finance Act 1986 which could lead to the Company or any Subsidiary incurring such a liability or becoming so accountable.

18.6   The Sale Shares are not chargeable securities for the purposes of section 99 of the Finance Act 1986.

18.7   Neither the Company nor any Subsidiary is, or has been, a person falling within subsections (6), (7) or (8) of section 67 or section 70 of the Finance Act 1986. None of them has given, or is obliged to give, any notification under section 68 or section 71 of the Finance Act 1986 or incurred any liability to stamp duty reserve tax under sections 93-97, of the Finance Act 1986.

19   TAX SHARING

Neither the Company nor any Subsidiary is bound by or party to any Taxation indemnity, Taxation sharing or any Taxation allocation agreement in respect of which claims against the Company or any Subsidiary would not be time barred.

20   CONSTRUCTION INDUSTRY SUB-CONTRACTORS' SCHEME

Neither the Company nor any Subsidiary is required to register as a Contractor under the provisions of section 59 of the Finance Act 2004 and the expenditure incurred by each of the Company and any Subsidiary on construction, refurbishment and fitting-out works in each of the three years ending on the Accounting Date is less than £1 million.

SCHEDULE 6

TAX COVENANT

1   INTERPRETATION

1.1   The definitions and rules of interpretation in this paragraph apply in this Tax Covenant.

Buyer's Relief: means:

(a) any Accounts Relief (as defined in paragraph (a) of the definition of Liability for Taxation) or Repayment Relief (as defined in paragraph (b) of the definition of Liability for Taxation),

(b) any Post-[Accounts Date OR Completion] Relief of the Company or any Subsidiary (as defined in paragraph (c) of the definition of Liability for Taxation), and

(c) any Relief, whenever arising, of the Buyer or any member of the Buyer's Tax Group other than the Company or any Subsidiary.

Buyer's Tax Group: the Buyer and any other company or companies which either are or become after Completion, or have within the seven years ending at Completion, been treated as members of the same group as, or otherwise connected or associated in any way with, the Buyer for any Tax purpose.

Event: includes (without limitation) the expiry of a period of time, the Company or any Subsidiary becoming or ceasing to be associated with any other person for any Tax purpose or ceasing to be or becoming resident in any country for any Tax purpose, the death or the winding up or dissolution of any person, and any transaction (including the execution and completion of all provisions of this agreement), event, act or omission whatsoever, and any reference to an Event occurring on or before a particular date shall include Events which, for Tax purposes, are deemed to have, or are treated or regarded as having, occurred on or before that date.

Liability for Taxation: any liability of the Company or a Subsidiary to make a payment of or in respect of Tax, whether or not the same is primarily payable by the Company or the relevant Subsidiary and whether or not the Company or the relevant Subsidiary has or may have any right of reimbursement against any other person or persons and also includes:

(a) the Loss of any Relief (Accounts Relief) where such Relief has been taken into account in computing and so reducing or eliminating any provision for deferred Tax which appears in the [Accounts OR Completion Accounts] (or which, but for such Relief, would have appeared in the [Accounts OR Completion Accounts]) or where such Relief was treated as an asset of the Company or the relevant Subsidiary in the [Accounts OR Completion Accounts] or was taken into account in computing any deferred Tax asset which appears in the [Accounts OR Completion Accounts] (Loss of an Accounts Relief), in which case the amount of the Liability for Taxation shall be the amount of Tax which would (on the basis of Tax rates current at the date of such Loss) have been saved but for such Loss, assuming for this purpose that the Company or the relevant Subsidiary had sufficient profits or was otherwise in a position to use the Relief,

(b) the Loss of any right to repayment of Tax (including any repayment supplement) (Repayment Relief) which was treated as an asset in the [Accounts OR Completion Accounts] (Loss of a Repayment Relief), in which case the amount of the Liability for Taxation shall be the amount of the Loss of the right to repayment and any related repayment supplement,

(c) the set off or use against income, profits or gains earned, accrued or received or against any Tax chargeable in respect of an Event occurring on or before [the Accounts Date OR Completion] of any Relief (Post-[Accounts Date OR Completion] Relief) or right to repayment of Tax (including any repayment supplement) which is not available before [the Accounts Date OR Completion], but arises after [the Accounts Date OR Completion] in circumstances where, but for such set off or use, the Company or the relevant Subsidiary would have had a liability to make a payment of or in respect of Tax for which the Buyer would have been able to make a claim against the Sellers under this Tax Covenant (Loss of a Post-[Accounts Date OR Completion] Relief), in which case the amount of the Liability for Taxation shall be the amount of Tax saved by the Company or the relevant Subsidiary as a result of such set off or use, and

(d) any liability of the Company or any Subsidiary to make a payment pursuant to an indemnity, guarantee or covenant entered into before Completion under which the Company or the relevant Subsidiary has agreed to meet or pay a sum equivalent to or by reference to another person's Tax liability, in which case the Liability for Taxation shall be equal to the amount of the liability.

Loss: any reduction, modification, loss, counteraction, nullification, utilisation, disallowance or clawback for whatever reason.

[Overprovision: the amount by which any provision in the [Accounts OR Completion Accounts] relating to Tax (other than a provision for deferred Tax) is overstated (except to the extent that such overstatement results from the utilisation of a Buyer's Relief), applying the accounting policies, principles and practices adopted in relation to the preparation of the [Accounts OR Completion Accounts] (and ignoring the effect of any change in law made after Completion).]

Relief: includes any loss, relief, allowance, credit, exemption or set off in respect of Tax or any deduction in computing income, profits or gains for the purposes of Tax and any right to a repayment of Tax.

Saving: the reduction or elimination of any liability of the Company or a Subsidiary to make an actual payment of corporation tax in respect of which the Sellers would not have been liable under paragraph 2, by the use of any Relief arising wholly as a result of a Liability for Taxation in respect of which the Sellers have made a payment under paragraph 2 of this Tax Covenant.

Tax: all forms of taxation and statutory, governmental, state, federal, provincial, local, government or municipal charges, duties, imposts, contributions, levies, withholdings or liabilities wherever chargeable and whether of the UK or any other

	jurisdiction, and any penalty, fine, surcharge, interest, charges or costs relating thereto, and Taxation shall have the same meaning.
Tax Claim:	any assessment (including self-assessment), notice, demand, letter or other document issued or action taken by or on behalf of any Taxation Authority from which it appears that the Buyer, the Company or a Subsidiary is or may be subject to a Liability for Taxation or other liability in respect of which the Sellers are or may be liable under this Tax Covenant.
Taxation Authority:	any government, state or municipality or any local, state, federal or other fiscal, revenue, customs or excise authority, body or official competent to impose, administer, levy, assess or collect Tax in the United Kingdom or elsewhere.
Taxation Statute:	any directive, statute, enactment, law or regulation wheresoever enacted or issued, coming into force or entered into providing for or imposing any Tax and including orders, regulations, instruments, bye-laws or other subordinate legislation made under the relevant statute or statutory provision and any directive, statute, enactment, law, order, regulation or provision which amends, extends, consolidates or replaces the same or which has been amended, extended, consolidated or replaced by the same.

1.2 References to gross receipts, income, profits or gains earned, accrued or received shall include any gross receipts, income, profits or gains deemed pursuant to the relevant Taxation Statute to have been or treated or regarded as earned, accrued or received.

1.3 References to a repayment of Tax shall include any repayment supplement or interest in respect of it.

1.4 [A reference to an Event occurring on or before Completion includes a series or combination of Events[, all of which were or the first of which was an Event occurring on or before Completion or which commenced on or before Completion OR the first of which occurred on or before Completion and was not in the ordinary course of business of the Company or the relevant Subsidiary and any of which occurring after Completion were in the ordinary course of business of the Company or the relevant Subsidiary].]

1.5 Any reference to something occurring in the ordinary course of business shall, without prejudice to the generality thereof, be deemed not to include:

    1.5.1 anything which involves, or leads directly or indirectly to, any liability of the Company or the relevant Subsidiary to Tax that is the primary liability of, or properly attributable to, or due from another person (other than a member of the Buyer's Tax Group), or is the liability of the Company or the relevant Subsidiary only because some other person, other than a member of the Buyer's Tax Group, has failed to pay it or is the liability of the Company or the relevant Subsidiary because it has elected to be regarded as taxable or liable or to be regarded as having made a disposal, or

1.5.2   anything which relates to or involves the acquisition or disposal of an asset or the supply of services (including the lending of money, or the hiring or licensing of tangible or intangible property) in a transaction which is not entered into on arm's length terms, or

1.5.3   anything which relates to or involves the making of a distribution for Tax purposes, the creation, cancellation or re-organisation of share or loan capital, the creation, cancellation or repayment of any intra-Group debt or the Company or any Subsidiary becoming or ceasing to be or being treated as ceasing to be a member of a Group or as becoming or ceasing to be associated or connected with any other company for any Tax purposes, or

1.5.4   anything which relates to a transaction or arrangement which includes, or a series of transactions or arrangements which include, any step or steps having no commercial or business purpose apart from the reduction, avoidance or deferral of a Liability for Taxation, or

1.5.5   anything which gives rise to a Liability for Taxation on deemed (as opposed to actual) profits or to the extent that it gives rise to a Liability for Taxation on an amount of profits greater than the difference between the sale proceeds of an asset and the amount attributable to that asset in the Accounts or, in the case of an asset acquired since the Accounts Date, the cost of that asset, or

1.5.6   anything which involves, or leads directly or indirectly to, a change of residence of the Company or any of the Subsidiaries for Tax purposes.

1.6   Unless the contrary intention appears, words and expressions defined in this agreement have the same meaning in this Tax Covenant and any provisions in this agreement concerning matters of construction or interpretation also apply in this Tax Covenant.

2   COVENANT

2.1   The Sellers covenant with the Buyer that, subject to the provisions of this Tax Covenant, the Sellers shall be [jointly and severally] liable to pay to the Buyer by way of repayment of the Purchase Price for the Sale Shares, to the extent possible but not so as to limit the amount payable where not wholly possible, an amount equal to any:

2.1.1   Liability for Taxation resulting from or by reference to any Event occurring on or before Completion or in respect of any gross receipts, income, profits or gains earned, accrued or received by the Company or any of the Subsidiaries on or before Completion,

2.1.2   Liability for Taxation which arises solely as a result of the relationship for Tax purposes of the Company or any of the Subsidiaries with any person other than a member of the Buyer's Tax Group whensoever arising,

2.1.3　any Liability for Taxation falling within paragraph (a) to paragraph (d) of the definition of Liability for Taxation,

2.1.4　any Liability for Taxation which is a liability for inheritance tax which:

　　　2.1.4.1　arises as a result of a transfer of value occurring or being deemed to occur on or before Completion (whether or not in conjunction with the death of any person whensoever occurring), or

　　　2.1.4.2　has given rise at Completion to a charge on any of the Sale Shares or assets of the Company or any of the Subsidiaries, or

　　　2.1.4.3　gives rise after Completion to a charge on any of the Sale Shares in or assets of the Company or any of the Subsidiaries as a result of the death of any person within seven years of a transfer of value which occurred before Completion, [and]

2.1.5　[any Liability for Tax arising in connection with or as a result of [SPECIFIC TAX ISSUE(S) ARISING FROM DUE DILIGENCE], and]

2.1.6　costs and expenses referred to in paragraph 11.

2.2　For the purposes of this Tax Covenant, in determining whether a charge on the shares in or assets of the Company or any of the Subsidiaries arises at any time or whether there is a liability for inheritance tax, the fact that any Tax may be paid in instalments shall be disregarded and such Tax shall be treated for the purposes of this Tax Covenant as becoming due or to have become due and a charge as arising or having arisen on the date of the transfer of value or other date or Event on or in respect of which it becomes payable or arises.

2.3　The provisions of section 213 of IHTA 1984 (refund by instalments) shall be deemed not to apply to any liability for inheritance tax falling within this paragraph 2.

3　PAYMENT DATE AND INTEREST

3.1　Where the Sellers are liable to make any payment under paragraph 2 (including any payment pursuant to paragraph 2.1.6), the due date for the making of that payment (Due Date) shall be the earlier of the date falling [seven] days after the Buyer has served a notice on the Sellers demanding that payment and in a case:

　　3.1.1　that involves an actual payment of Tax by the Company or any of the Subsidiaries (including any payment pursuant to paragraph 2.1.6), the date on which the Tax in question would have had to have been paid to the relevant Taxation Authority in order to prevent a liability to interest or a fine, surcharge or penalty from arising in respect of the Liability for Taxation in question, or

　　3.1.2　that falls within paragraph (a) of the definition of Liability for Taxation, the last date on which the Tax is or would have been required to be paid to the relevant Taxation Authority in respect of the period in which the Loss of the Relief occurs (assuming for this purpose that the Company or the relevant Subsidiary had sufficient profits or was otherwise in a position to use the Relief), or

3.1.3   that falls within paragraph (b) of the definition of Liability for Taxation, the date on which the repayment was due from the relevant Taxation Authority, or

3.1.4   that falls within paragraph (c) of the definition of Liability for Taxation, the date on which the Tax saved by the Company or the relevant Subsidiary is or would have been required to be paid to the relevant Taxation Authority, or

3.1.5   that falls within paragraph (d) of the definition of Liability for Taxation not later than the fifth day before the day on which the Company or the relevant Subsidiary is due to make the payment or repayment.

3.2   Any dispute as to the amount specified in any notice served on the Sellers under paragraph 3.1.2 to paragraph 3.1.5 shall be determined by the auditors of the Company or the relevant Subsidiary for the time being, acting as experts and not as arbitrators (the costs of that determination being shared equally by the Sellers and the Buyer).

3.3   If any sums required to be paid by the Sellers under this Tax Covenant are not paid on the Due Date then, except to the extent that the Sellers' liability under paragraph 2 compensates the Buyer for the late payment by virtue of it extending to interest and penalties, such sums shall bear interest (which shall accrue from day to day after as well as before any judgment for the same) at the rate of [2]% per annum over the base rate from time to time of [NAME OF BANK] or (in the absence thereof) at such similar rate as the Buyer selects from the day following the Due Date up to and including the day of actual payment of such sums, such interest to be compounded quarterly.

4   EXCLUSIONS

4.1   The covenant contained in paragraph 2 shall not cover any Liability for Taxation to the extent that:

4.1.1   a provision or reserve in respect thereof is made in the [Accounts OR Completion Accounts], or

4.1.2   [it arises as a result of a transaction in the ordinary course of business of the Company or any of the Subsidiaries between the Accounts Date and Completion and is not an interest or penalty, surcharge or fine in connection with Tax], or

4.1.3   it arises or is increased as a result only of any change in the law of Tax announced and coming into force after Completion (whether relating to rates of Tax or otherwise) or the withdrawal of any extra-statutory concession previously made by a Taxation Authority (whether or not the change purports to be effective retrospectively in whole or in part), or

4.1.4   it would not have arisen but for a change after Completion in the accounting bases on which the Company or any of the Subsidiaries values its assets (other than a change made in order to comply with UK GAAP), or

4.1.5   the Buyer is compensated for any such matter under any other provision of this agreement, or

4.1.6   it would not have arisen but for a voluntary act or transaction carried out by the Buyer, the Company or any of the Subsidiaries after Completion, being an act which:

     4.1.6.1   is not in the ordinary course of business, or

     4.1.6.2   could reasonably have been avoided, or

     4.1.6.3   the Company or the relevant Subsidiary was not legally committed to do under a commitment that existed on or before Completion, or

     4.1.6.4   the Buyer was aware would give rise to the Liability for Taxation in question.

4.2   [The provisions of paragraph 4.1 of this Tax Covenant [and clause 7.2 to clause 7.6] (limits on the amount of recovery) of this agreement] shall not apply to any claims in respect of any Liability for Taxation falling within paragraph 2.1.5 of this Tax Covenant.

5   [OVERPROVISIONS

5.1   If, on or before the seventh anniversary of Completion, the auditors for the time being of the Company or any of the Subsidiaries certify (at the request and expense of the Sellers) that any provision for Tax in the [Accounts OR Completion Accounts] has proved to be an Overprovision, then:

     5.1.1   the amount of any Overprovision shall first be set off against any payment then due from the Sellers under this Tax Covenant,

     5.1.2   to the extent that there is an excess, a refund shall be made to the Sellers of any previous payment or payments made by the Sellers under this Tax Covenant (and not previously refunded under this Tax Covenant) up to the amount of such excess, and

     5.1.3   to the extent that such excess as referred to in paragraph 5.1.2 is not exhausted, the remainder of that excess shall be carried forward and set off against any future payment or payments which become due from the Sellers under this Tax Covenant.

5.2   After the Company's or the relevant Subsidiary's auditors have produced any certificate under this paragraph 5, the Sellers or the Buyer may, at any time before the seventh anniversary of Completion, request the auditors for the time being of the Company or the relevant Subsidiary (as the case may be) to review (at the expense of the Sellers) that certificate in the light of all relevant circumstances, including any facts of which they were not or it was not aware, and which were not taken into account, at the time when such certificate was produced and to certify whether, in their opinion, the certificate remains correct or whether, in light of those circumstances, it should be amended.

5.3   If the auditors make an amendment to the earlier certificate and the amount of the Overprovision is revised, that revised amount shall be substituted for the previous amount and any adjusting payment that is required shall be made by or to the Sellers (as the case may be) as soon as reasonably practicable.]

6   SAVINGS

If (at the Sellers' request and expense) the auditors for the time being of the Company or any Subsidiary determine that the Company or the relevant Subsidiary has obtained a Saving, the Buyer shall, as soon as reasonably practicable thereafter, repay to the Sellers the lesser of:

6.1.1   the amount of the Saving (as determined by the auditors) less any costs incurred by the Buyer, the Company or the relevant Subsidiary, and

6.1.2   the amount paid by the Sellers under paragraph 2 in respect of the Liability for Taxation which gave rise to the Saving less any part of that amount previously repaid to the Sellers under any provision of this Tax Covenant or otherwise.

7   RECOVERY FROM THIRD PARTIES

7.1   Where the Sellers have paid an amount in full discharge of a liability under paragraph 2 in respect of any Liability for Taxation and the Buyer, the Company or any of the Subsidiaries is or becomes entitled to recover from some other person (not being the Buyer, the Company or any of the Subsidiaries or any other company within the Buyer's Tax Group), any amount in respect of such Liability for Taxation, the Buyer shall or shall procure that the Company or the relevant Subsidiary shall:

7.1.1   notify the Sellers of its entitlement as soon as reasonably practicable, and

7.1.2   if required by the Sellers and, subject to the Buyer, the Company or the relevant Subsidiary being [secured and] indemnified by the Sellers against any Tax that may be suffered on receipt of that amount and any costs and expenses incurred in recovering that amount, take or procure that the Company or the relevant Subsidiary takes all reasonable steps to enforce that recovery against the person in question (keeping the Sellers fully informed of the progress of any action taken), provided that the Buyer shall not be required to take any action pursuant to this paragraph 7.1 [(other than an action against:

7.1.2.1 a Taxation Authority, or

7.1.2.2 a person who has given Tax advice to the Company or relevant Subsidiary on or before Completion)],

which, in the Buyer's reasonable opinion, is likely to harm its, the Company's or the relevant Subsidiary's commercial relationship (potential or actual) with that or any other person.

7.2   If the Buyer, the Company or any of the Subsidiaries recovers any amount referred to in paragraph 7.1, the Buyer shall account to the Sellers for the lesser of:

7.2.1   any amount recovered (including any related interest or related repayment supplement) less any Tax suffered in respect of that amount and any costs and expenses incurred in recovering that amount (save to the extent that amount has already been made good by the Sellers under paragraph 7.1.2), and

7.2.2   the amount paid by the Sellers under paragraph 2 in respect of the Liability for Taxation in question.

8   CORPORATION TAX RETURNS

8.1   The Sellers or their duly authorised agent shall, at the Sellers' cost and expense, prepare the corporation tax returns and computations of the Company and the Subsidiaries for all accounting periods ended on or before the Accounts Date, to the extent that the same have not been prepared before Completion, and submit them to the Buyer.

8.2   The Buyer shall procure that the returns and computations referred to in paragraph 8.1 shall be authorised, signed and submitted to the relevant Taxation Authority without amendment or with such amendments as the Buyer reasonably considers to be necessary and shall give the Sellers or their agent all such assistance as may reasonably be required (at the Sellers' cost and expense) to agree those returns and computations with the relevant Taxation Authority, provided that the Buyer shall not be obliged to take any such action as is mentioned in this paragraph 8.2 in relation to any return that is not full, true and accurate in all material respects.

8.3   The Sellers or their duly authorised agent shall, at the Sellers' cost and expense, prepare all documentation and shall have conduct of all matters (including correspondence) relating to the corporation tax returns and computations of the Company and the Subsidiaries for all accounting periods ended on or prior to the Accounts Date, provided that the Sellers shall not, without the prior written consent of the Buyer (not to be unreasonably withheld or delayed), transmit any communication (written or otherwise) to the relevant Taxation Authority or agree any matter with the relevant Taxation Authority.

8.4   The Buyer shall procure that the Company and the Subsidiaries, at the Sellers' cost and expense, afford such access to their books, accounts and records as is necessary and reasonable to enable the Sellers or their duly authorised agent to prepare the corporation tax returns and computations of the Company and the Subsidiaries for all accounting periods ended on or before the Accounts Date and conduct matters relating to them in accordance with this paragraph 8.

8.5   The Sellers shall take all reasonable steps to ensure that the corporation tax returns and computations of the Company and the Subsidiaries for all accounting periods ended on or before the Accounts Date are prepared and agreed with the relevant Taxation Authority as soon as possible.

8.6   For the avoidance of doubt:

8.6.1   where any matter relating to Tax gives rise to a Tax Claim, the provisions of paragraph 9 shall take precedence over the provisions of this paragraph 8, and

8.6.2   the provisions of this paragraph 8 shall not prejudice the rights of the Buyer to make a Tax Claim under this Tax Covenant in respect of any Liability for Taxation.

9   CONDUCT OF TAX CLAIMS

9.1   If the Buyer, the Company or any of the Subsidiaries becomes aware of a Tax Claim, the Buyer shall give or procure that notice in writing is given to the Sellers as soon as is reasonably practicable, provided that if any of the Sellers receive any Tax Claim for whatever reason, they shall notify the Buyer in writing as soon as is reasonably practicable and the Buyer shall be deemed, on receipt of such notification, to have given the Sellers notice of such Tax Claim in accordance with the provisions of this paragraph 9, provided always that the giving of such notice shall not be a condition precedent to the Sellers' liability under this Tax Covenant.

9.2   Provided the Sellers indemnify [and secure] the Buyer and the Company or the relevant Subsidiary to the Buyer's reasonable satisfaction against all liabilities, costs, damages or expenses which may be incurred thereby including any additional Liability for Taxation, the Buyer shall take and shall procure that the Company or the relevant Subsidiary shall take such action as the Sellers may reasonably request by notice in writing given to the Buyer, the Company or the relevant Subsidiary to avoid, dispute, defend, resist, appeal or compromise any Tax Claim (such a Tax Claim where action is so requested being hereinafter referred to as a Dispute), provided that neither the Buyer, the Company nor the relevant Subsidiary shall be obliged to appeal or procure an appeal against any assessment to Tax raised on any of them if, the Sellers having been given written notice of the receipt of such assessment, the Buyer, the Company or the relevant Subsidiary have not within [14] days of the date of the notice received instructions in writing from the Sellers to do so.

9.3   If:

9.3.1   the Sellers do not request the Buyer, the Company or the relevant Subsidiary to take any action under paragraph 9.2 or fail to indemnify [and secure] the Buyer, the Company or the relevant Subsidiary to the Buyer's reasonable satisfaction within a period of time (commencing with the date of the notice given to the Sellers) that is reasonable, having regard to the nature of the Tax Claim and the existence of any time limit in relation to avoiding, disputing, defending, resisting, appealing or compromising such Tax Claim, and which period shall not in any event exceed a period of [14] days, or

9.3.2   any of the Sellers (or the Company or the relevant Subsidiary before Completion) has been involved in a case involving fraudulent conduct or wilful default in respect of the Liability for Taxation which is the subject matter of the Dispute, or

9.3.3   the Dispute involves an appeal against a determination by the Tax Chamber of the First-tier Tribunal (or, for appeals lodged before 1 April 2009, a determination by the General or Special Commissioners or the VAT and Duties Tribunal) unless the Sellers have obtained the opinion of Tax counsel of at least [5] years' standing that there is a reasonable prospect that the appeal will succeed,

the Buyer, the Company or the relevant Subsidiary shall have the conduct of the Dispute absolutely (without prejudice to its rights under this Tax Covenant) and shall be free to pay or settle the Tax Claim on such terms as the Buyer, the Company or the relevant Subsidiary may in its absolute discretion considers fit.

9.4   Subject to paragraph 9.3, by agreement in writing between the Buyer and the Sellers, the conduct of a Dispute may be delegated to the Sellers on such terms as may be agreed from time to time between the Buyer and the Sellers provided that, unless the Buyer and the Sellers specifically agree otherwise in writing, the following terms shall be deemed to be incorporated into any such agreement:

9.4.1   the Buyer, the Company or the relevant Subsidiary shall promptly be kept fully informed of all matters pertaining to a Dispute and shall be entitled to see and keep copies of all correspondence and notes or other written records of telephone conversations or meetings and, in the event that there is no written record, shall be given an immediate report of all telephone conversations with any Taxation Authority to the extent that it relates to a Dispute,

9.4.2   the appointment of solicitors or other professional advisers shall be subject to the written approval of the Buyer, such approval not to be unreasonably withheld or delayed,

9.4.3   all material written communications pertaining to the Dispute which are to be transmitted to the relevant Taxation Authority shall first be submitted to the Buyer, the Company or the relevant Subsidiary for approval and shall only be finally transmitted if such approval is given, such approval not to be unreasonably withheld or delayed, and

9.4.4   the Sellers shall make no settlement or compromise of the Dispute or agree any matter in the conduct of the Dispute which is likely to affect the amount thereof or the future liability to Tax of the Buyer, the Company or any relevant Subsidiary without the prior approval of the Buyer, the Company or the relevant Subsidiary (as may be appropriate), such approval not to be unreasonably withheld or delayed.

9.5   The Buyer shall provide and shall procure that the Company or relevant Subsidiary provides to the Sellers and the Sellers' professional advisors reasonable access to premises and personnel and to any relevant assets, documents and records within their power, possession or control for the purpose of investigating the matter and enabling the Sellers to take such action as is referred to in this paragraph 9,

9.6   Neither the Buyer, the Company nor any of the Subsidiaries shall be subject to any claim by or liability to any of the Sellers for non-compliance with any of the foregoing provisions of this paragraph 9 if the Buyer, the Company or any of the Subsidiaries has bona fide acted in accordance with the instructions of any one or more of the Sellers.

10   GROSSING UP

10.1   All sums payable by the Sellers to the Buyer under this Tax Covenant shall be paid free and clear of all deductions or withholdings whatsoever unless the deduction or withholding is required by law.   If any deductions or withholdings are required by law to be made from any of the sums payable under this Tax Covenant, the Sellers shall pay to the Buyer such sum as will, after the deduction or withholding has been made, leave the Buyer with the same amount as it would have been entitled to receive in the absence of any such requirement to make a deduction or withholding.

10.2   If the Buyer incurs a taxation liability which results from, or is calculated by reference to, any sum paid under this Tax Covenant, the amount so payable shall be increased by such amount as will ensure that, after payment of the taxation liability, the Buyer is left with a net sum equal to the sum it would have received had no such taxation liability arisen.

10.3   If the Buyer would, but for the availability of a Buyer's Relief, incur a taxation liability falling within paragraph 10.2, it shall be deemed for the purposes of that paragraph to have incurred and paid that liability.

10.4   [If the Buyer assigns the benefit of this Tax Covenant or this agreement, the Sellers shall not be liable pursuant to paragraph 10.1 or paragraph 10.2, save to the extent that the Sellers would have been so liable had no such assignment occurred.]

11   COSTS AND EXPENSES

The covenant contained in paragraph 2 of this Tax Covenant shall extend to all costs and expenses incurred by the Buyer, the Company or any of the Subsidiaries in connection with any matter included under paragraph 2 of this Tax Covenant and the enforcement of rights under this Tax Covenant.

SCHEDULE 7
INTELLECTUAL PROPERTY RIGHTS

Part 1 - Registered Intellectual Property Rights

Part 2 - Material unregistered Intellectual Property Rights

Part 3 - Intellectual Property Rights licensed from third parties

Part 4 - Intellectual Property Rights licensed to third parties

SCHEDULE 8
INFORMATION TECHNOLOGY

Part 1 - Particulars of IT system

Part 2 - Particulars of IT contracts

SCHEDULE 9
PARTICULARS OF PROPERTIES

Part 1 - Freehold Properties

Description of the Property	
Owner	
Registered/unregistered (and title number)	
Occupier	
Current Use	
Is there an Investment Lease?	
Tenant under an Investment Lease	
Contractual date of termination of Investment Lease.	

Part 2 - Leasehold Properties

Description of the Property	
Description of Lease (lease, underlease, licence, date and parties)	
Owner	
Registered/unregistered (and title number)	
Contractual date of termination of lease	
Occupier	
Current Use	
Is there an Investment Lease?	
Tenant under an Investment Lease	
Contractual date of termination of Investment Lease	

Signed by [NAME OF SELLER] ....

Signed by [NAME OF SELLER] ....

Signed by [NAME OF SELLER] ....

Signed by [NAME OF DIRECTOR]
for and on behalf of [NAME OF BUYER] ....
Director

Appendix VII

Capital Gains Tax
Enterprise Investment Scheme Deferral Relief

Trading activities not eligible for relief

a) Any activity that is not commercially undertaken with a view to profit.

b) Dealing in land, in commodities or futures, or in shares, securities or other financial instruments.

c) Property backed ventures such as hotels, nursing homes, farming and property development.

d) Dealing in goods other than in the course of an ordinary trade of wholesale or retail distribution.

e) Banking, insurance, money-lending, debt-factoring, hire purchase financing or other financial activities.

f) Most leasing (including ship chartering) or receiving royalties or licence fees.

g) Providing legal or accounting services.

h) Providing services or facilities for a trade carried on by someone else (other than its holding company) whose activities consist, to a substantial extent, of activities within (b) to (g) and a controlling interest in whose trade is held by a person who has a controlling interest in the trade of the company providing the services or facilities.

Appendix VIII

Glossary

Alternative Investment Market (AIM)
A stock exchange for smaller companies. Has less regulation than the London Stock Exchange.

Asset-stripping
Buying a company, and then selling its surplus assets to produce an overall profit on the transaction. Sometimes the parts of a business are worth more than the whole.

Banker's draft
A guaranteed cheque issued by and in the name of a bank which cannot be cancelled. As good as cash.

BIMBO
Buy-In Management Buy Out: A combined MBI and MBO.

Completion
The time when the Sale and Purchase Agreement becomes effective and the purchaser owns the company.

Completion meeting
Where the seller and purchaser meet with their respective solicitors to effect the Sale and Purchase Agreement – not a simple affair, this can often take a whole day or more.

Confidentiality undertaking
An agreement by prospective purchasers to keep confidential any information they may receive on your business and not to use it except in evaluating your business. It also usually includes an undertaking to return any information when requested to do so and confirm that no copies have been made. It sometimes contains an indemnity for damages resulting from unauthorised use. However, in practice these rights can be difficult to enforce.

Consideration
The total amount you are receiving for the sale of the business. It may include a non-cash element, such as shares in the acquiring company.

Contingent consideration
Where part of the total price of your business is dependent on a specific event, usually profitability (see Earn out), but could be the renewal of a major contract or the outcome of litigation etc.

Deferred consideration

Where part of the total price of your business is paid at a future date.

Disclosure Letter
A document prepared by you and your solicitor detailing specific facts about the business so that in the future the purchaser cannot claim no knowledge of them.

Dividend strip
Payment of a dividend before selling, either to reduce the price paid by the purchaser or to maximise the net of tax receipts of the vendor.

Due diligence
The investigation into your company's affairs by the purchaser or his financiers. Usually undertaken by accountants and solicitors.

Earn-out
Where part of the price you receive for your business is dependent upon the size of future profits.

Earnings per share (EPS)
The after tax profit of a company divided by the number of shares in issue.

Engrossment
Final, fully agreed, bound Sale and Purchase Agreement ready for signature.

Equity
The share capital of a company or the value belonging to the shareholders.

Gearing
Level of borrowings of a business in relation to equity.

Goodwill
The price paid for a business above the value of its net assets.

Heads of Agreement
An outline of the main points agreed between the vendor and the purchaser. May or may not be binding.

Hive-down
Transferring selected assets or activities of a company to a new subsidiary. Usually, the subsidiary is then sold.

Indemnities and Warranties
A legally binding guarantee that specific information you have given the purchaser about your business is not false or incomplete.

Information Memorandum
A document designed to give a prospective purchaser enough information on your business to decide whether to proceed. A selling document.

Leveraged buyout

Buying a business using a lot of borrowed money.

Loan notes
A formal loan agreement, usually with pre-set repayment dates, with a specified rate of interest.

Lock-out
An agreement with a prospective buyer not to proceed with negotiation/sale to anyone else for a specified period.

Mezzanine finance
High risk lending, usually fairly short term where the lender does not have a first charge or debenture. In return, he expects a high rate of interest and usually, some kind of equity interest.

MBI
Management buy-in. Where an individual or a team of people buy a business to run it themselves, usually with a lot of borrowed money.

MBO
Management buy-out. Where the business is sold to the existing management, usually with a lot of borrowed money.

Net assets
The value of all the assets of a business less all its liabilities. Also known as Shareholders' funds.

P/E ratio
Price/earnings ratio: a shorthand way of assessing the value of the business in terms of the number of years it takes to recover the purchase price out of its after-tax profits.

PLUS
A type of Stock Exchange buying and selling shares on a matched deal basis. Formerly known as OFEX.

Prospectus
See Information Memorandum. Can mean a formal document prepared in accordance with the Financial Services and Markets Act 2000.

Reinvestment Relief
The reinvesting of a capital gain into shares in an eligible trading business so as to defer payment of capital gains tax.

Reporting accountants
The accountants employed by the prospective purchaser to undertake due diligence (q.v.) and to report thereon.

Restrictive covenants
Typically, your agreement not to compete for an agreed period with the business you

have sold.

Rollover relief
Deferring part or all of the capital gains tax on the sale of a business by accepting shares or loan stock in the acquiring company instead of cash.

Sale and Purchase Agreement
The legally binding document detailing the agreement between the seller and the purchaser: it sets out who is selling what to whom for how much and when.

Senior debt
Bank or similar loans where the lender has a first charge or debenture.

Shareholders' funds
See Net assets.

Vendor finance
Where the seller agrees to loan back to the company some of the sale proceeds or accept deferred consideration.

Vendor placing
Where the purchaser, which is a quoted company, issues its own shares for an acquisition which are immediately sold on the Stock Exchange to produce the agreed cash price for the seller

Venture capital
Investment capital, typically offered with low security but requiring a high anticipated rate of return.

Appendix IX

McIntyre Hudson Corporate Finance Limited

Authorised and regulated by the Financial Services Authority, MacIntyre Hudson Corporate Finance Limited provides a full range of corporate finance services tailored specifically to each individual client's needs. We work closely with our clients to identify their key corporate goals and then we devise a strategy to achieve those goals. Our aim is to help our clients to remain focused on their day-to-day business activities whilst we guide them through the complexities of a deal.

Disposals

We specialise in the disposal of UK and international companies. We work closely with clients to maximise the value of the business prior to sale. Having produced an appropriate information memorandum on the business, we use our industry contacts to identify and develop a list of buyers that are suitable to achieve your objectives.

Our role then moves on to the negotiation stage when we give advice on all aspects of the transaction. Structuring the actual deal is a crucial part of our disposal work and it is particularly important to ensure that clients receive the right tax advice.

We give you a total "hand-holding" service from the initial stages right through to the final signing and we are always there to provide professional (and emotional!) support throughout the sale. We recognise that this is probably the most important financial transaction of your life and it has got to be right.

Acquisitions

Growing your business organically is not the only option. We can help you make successful business acquisitions. Starting with a review of your corporate strategy, we then identify and value target companies, negotiate the price, structure the deal, source the required finance and advise on the taxation issues, so that you achieve the optimal result with the right deal structure in place. Throughout the process, we will represent your interests during negotiations with the financiers, the vendors and their advisers.

Fund raising

Securing the right type of finance as you grow your business is crucial. We will build up a detailed understanding of your corporate and personal objectives, and then focus on the key issues, putting together the right deal structure and finding the best financier for you. We work closely with numerous financial institutions and know exactly where to go to find just the right type of funding. We also assist you to negotiate the terms and conditions of the funding with the financiers and help with completion of the detailed contractual documentation.

Valuations

Whether you are looking to buy, sell or raise finance, we are able to value your business using our tried and tested methodology. Valuation is an art, not a science, and requires expert advice. We consider not only the asset base of the business but also its ability to generate cash and profit, so that the fair market value we determine is exactly that.

MBOs/MBIs

Few entrepreneurs carry out more than one or two MBOs during their working lives, so expert advice is essential. From the outset we will take responsibility for the day to day management of the transaction, identifying, analysing and finding solutions to the numerous complex issues which will arise, and ensuring delivery of a successful deal at a sensible price with an appropriate funding structure. We undertake an initial review of the commercial and financial feasibility of the deal and provide an indicative valuation of the business. We will then assist you to prepare a business plan and detailed financial projections. We will introduce you to appropriate financial backers and legal advisers, as well as negotiate the price with the vendors and the deal structure with the financiers.

Due Diligence

Due diligence establishes the soundness, or otherwise, of the target business you are acquiring. By carrying out a detailed review of the financial records of the target, we use our expertise and financial experience to verify that the business is all that it claims to be. This confirms previous representations made to you by the vendors and assists you and your other advisers with the ongoing negotiations as the deal nears completion.

IPOs

Floating your business can be an exhausting and complex process, so sound advice is key from the outset. We can help you groom your business for flotation and provide an indicative valuation for brokers. We also act as reporting accountant and tax adviser on the transaction. We will introduce you to the other professional advisers needed to make the transaction successful and to ensure that you comply with the many legal and regulatory requirements.

Strategic planning

Identifying and optimising the key strengths in your business will increase value. From the outset, it is essential to focus on key performance indicators and unique selling points. We help you to do this, probing how your business works so you can develop opportunities and minimise threats.

International capability

Our services are extended overseas via our membership of Morison International, a global association of independent accountants, auditors, tax advisers, business consultants and lawyers established to meet the cross-border needs of clients.

Member firms are experienced in dealing with cross-border assignments of different sizes and complexities. We work together under a common vision of world class customer service and the timely delivery of practical advice to clients.

www.morisoninternational.com

How to contact us

Our corporate finance services extend across the whole of the UK. If you would like to find out how your business could benefit from any of our corporate finance services, please visit www.macintyrehudson.co.uk or contact:

London City
Gary Morley
020 7429 4100
07973 334391
gary.morley@mhllp.co.uk

Milton Keynes
Laurence Whitehead
01908 662255
07769 740202
laurence.whitehead@mhllp.co.uk

High Wycombe
Cameron Cook
01494 441226
07979 517214
cameron.cook@mhllp.co.uk

We are a founder member of MHA, a fast growing UK wide association of respected and progressive independent accountants and business advisers, all sharing common values and goals.

www.mha-uk.com

Index